THE CAMBRIDGE BIBLE COMMENTARY

NEW ENGLISH BIBLE

GENERAL EDITORS
P. R. ACKROYD, A. R. C. LEANEY, J. W. PACKER

ACTS OF THE APOSTLES

ACTS OF THE APOSTLES

COMMENTARY BY

J. W. PACKER

Headmaster, Canon Slade Grammar School, Bolton

CAMBRIDGE
AT THE UNIVERSITY PRESS
1966

PUBLISHED BY
THE SYNDICS OF THE CAMBRIDGE UNIVERSITY PRESS

Bentley House, 200 Euston Road, London, N.W. 1
American Branch: 32 East 57th Street, New York, N.Y. 10022
West African Office: P.M.B. 5181, Ibadan, Nigeria

©

CAMBRIDGE UNIVERSITY PRESS

1966

Printed in Great Britain at the University Printing House, Cambridge
(Brooke Crutchley, University Printer)

LIBRARY OF CONGRESS CATALOGUE
CARD NUMBER: 66–13639

GENERAL EDITORS' PREFACE

The aim of this series is to provide the text of the New English Bible closely linked to a commentary in which the results of modern scholarship are made available to the general reader. Teachers and young people preparing for such examinations as the General Certificate of Education at Ordinary or Advanced Level in Britain, and for similar qualifications elsewhere, have been especially kept in mind. The commentators have been asked to assume no specialized theological knowledge, and no knowledge of Greek and Hebrew. Bare references to other literature and multiple references to other parts of the Bible have been avoided. Actual quotations have been given as often as possible.

Within these quite severe limits each commentator will attempt to set out the main findings of recent New Testament scholarship, and to describe the historical background to the text. The main theological content of the New Testament will also be critically discussed.

Much attention has been given to the form of the volumes. The aim is to produce books each of which will be read consecutively from first to last page. The introductory material leads naturally into the text, which itself leads into the alternating sections of commentary. By this means it is hoped that each book will be easily read and remain in the mind as a unity.

The series is prefaced by a volume—*Understanding the New Testament*—which outlines the larger historical background, says something about the growth and transmission of the text, and answers the question 'Why should we study the New Testament?' Another volume—*New Testament Illustrations*—contains maps, diagrams and photographs.

P. R. A.
A. R. C. L.
J. W. P.

EDITOR'S PREFACE

My dependence upon the work of many scholars will be obvious from a reading of this commentary and I am glad to express at once my gratitude and indebtedness to them. Perhaps twenty-five years' teaching experience in schools, colleges of education and universities has enabled me to appreciate to some degree the problems of young people who are studying the scriptures in detail, and to suggest lines of thought that may help them in their work. The text has been freely used in the commentary to enable it to speak for itself and so to avoid the danger, ever present to the student, of learning much about the scriptures rather than of studying them.

I am most grateful to Professor P. R. Ackroyd and Mr A. R. C. Leaney for all their help and encouragement and to the Cambridge University Press for its careful direction. Finally I should like to thank my wife for typing the original script and for her help in many other ways, and my family for its unwearying interest in this series.

J. W. P.

CONTENTS

MAPS AND PLANS

ROMAN EMPERORS

A.D. 14 Tiberius (Luke 3: 1–2)

37 Gaius, known as Caligula (Acts 9: 24 note, p. 74)

41 Claudius (Acts 18: 2)

54 Nero (Acts 25: 11–12)

GOVERNORS OF JUDAEA

A.D. 26 Pontius Pilate (Luke 23: 1–25)

36 Marcellus

37 Marullus

41 Herod Agrippa I (Acts 12: 1–23)

44 Cuspius Fadus

46 Tiberius Alexander

48 Ventidius Cumanus

52 Antonius Felix (Acts 23: 24 — 24: 27)

c. 59 Porcius Festus (Acts 25 and 26)

c. 61 Albinus

64 Gessius Florus

THE FAMILY OF HEROD THE GREAT IN ACTS

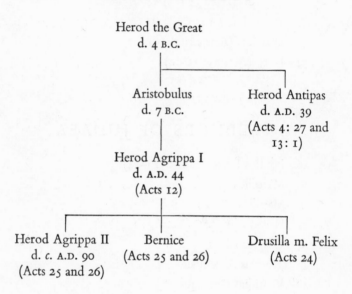

Herod the Great
d. 4 B.C.

Aristobulus
d. 7 B.C.

Herod Antipas
d. A.D. 39
(Acts 4: 27 and
13: 1)

Herod Agrippa I
d. A.D. 44
(Acts 12)

Herod Agrippa II
d. c. A.D. 90
(Acts 25 and 26)

Bernice
(Acts 25 and 26)

Drusilla m. Felix
(Acts 24)

ACTS

OF THE APOSTLES

✳   ✳   ✳   ✳   ✳   ✳   ✳   ✳   ✳   ✳   ✳   ✳   ✳

THE BOOK AND ITS AUTHOR

'And so to Rome' (Acts 28: 14)

'Acts of the Apostles' is a strange title for a book that says nothing at all about the majority of the apostles of Christ. Instead the scene is peopled with men and women from all over the Mediterranean world. 'There were at Antioch, in the congregation there, certain prophets and teachers: Barnabas, Simeon called Niger, Lucius of Cyrene, Manaen, who had been at the court of Prince Herod, and Saul' (13: 1). It is almost a missionary council or an international conference. Barnabas came from Cyprus, Simeon perhaps from Central Africa, Lucius from North Africa, Manaen from Palestine and Saul from Tarsus in Cilicia. Throughout this dramatic chronicle of the early church the stage is thronged. While a brief scene takes place between Philip the evangelist and the high official of the Ethiopian queen (8: 26–40), one of the principal actors, Saul of Tarsus, was 'breathing murderous threats against the disciples of the Lord' (9: 1). Sometimes an actor's part is played out and he leaves the stage for good: 'Barnabas took Mark with him and sailed for Cyprus' (15: 39). Immediately afterwards the gap is filled by a newcomer: 'he found a disciple named Timothy, the son of a Jewish Christian mother and a Greek father' (16: 1). The crowd is varied; the scene kaleidoscopic. Yet through the bustle of travellers and the noise of courts of law there stride the two principals, and so gigantic are they that there is scarcely room on the stage for them together. As soon as Peter escapes

I

from prison and leaves the scene, apart from his witness at the Jerusalem Council, Paul sets out from Antioch to conquer Asia Minor for the church.

This is not a first history of the early church, but a dramatic presentation, full of seething activity, of its formative years. B. H. Streeter in his *The Four Gospels* suggested that 'the title of the Acts might well have been "The Road to Rome"' (p. 532). Early Christianity followed the Roman roads but paused repeatedly by the way to convict and to convince. Perhaps, to adapt the title of Browning's poem, Acts tells 'how they brought the Good News from Jerusalem to Rome'. Indeed the apostles fulfilled Christ's command 'you will bear witness for me in Jerusalem, and all over Judaea and Samaria, and away to the ends of the earth' (1: 8).

'Greetings to you from our dear friend Luke, the doctor' (Col. 4: 14)

Luke's name is mentioned only three times in the New Testament. Paul sends Luke's greetings to the church at Colossae (Col. 4: 14). In writing to Timothy, Paul speaks of him as his companion: 'I have no one with me but Luke' (2 Tim. 4: 11), and writing to Philemon he refers to Luke with Mark, Aristarchus and Demas as one of his 'fellow-workers' (verse 24). That it was Luke who wrote Acts was the tradition of the church as early as the end of the second century A.D. Irenaeus, bishop of Lugdunum or Lyons in southern France, refers in *c.* 180–90 to the work as *The Acts of the Apostles* and its author as Luke. The Muratorian canon (a late second-century fragment discovered by Ludovico Antonio Muratori, archivist to the duke of Modena in Italy in the eighteenth century, and containing a list of New Testament books) calls the book *The Acts of All the Apostles* and assigns it to Luke. Similarly in a preface to the third Gospel, written at about the same time and known as 'the anti-Marcionite prologue', Luke is said to be the author of Acts as well as of the Gospel. This preface set out to discredit the teaching of Marcion (died *c.* 160) who had rejected the Old Testament and its influence in the New. It stated that Luke was a Syrian doctor from Antioch, a companion of Paul, who died unmarried at the age of 84 at Boeotia in central Greece.

The preface to Acts (1: 1–5) claims that the work is a continuation of the Gospel, and dedicated to Theophilus (see p. 21). The somewhat abrupt conclusion, leaving Paul in Rome for 'two full years at his own expense' (28: 30), may indicate that the author had projected a still further section covering the last phase of Paul's life, and culminating in his final imprisonment and death. Those sections in the latter half of the book in which the narrative changes from the third person to the first (16: 10–17; 20: 5–15; 21: 1–18; 27: 1—28: 16) may well be extracts from the author's travel-diary. As they start when Paul first leaves Asia for Europe and end in Rome, these 'we-sections' may imply that Luke first joined the party at Troas and then accompanied Paul on and off for the rest of his journeys (see below, p. 92, for reference to an earlier 'we-section' introduced in one manuscript at 11: 28). Sir William Ramsay's attractive suggestion (W. M. Ramsay, *St Paul the Traveller and the Roman Citizen*, p. 203) that Luke was himself the Macedonian (16: 9) whom Paul saw in his vision at Troas has not met with much support in view of the earlier tradition that Luke came from Antioch. Nonetheless it seems quite conceivable that a doctor from Antioch in Syria should have set up practice in so important a Roman town as Philippi and have met Paul on a visit to nearby Troas.

' *These men are servants of the Supreme God, and are declaring to you a way of salvation*' (Acts 16: 17)

The shout of the slave-girl in Philippi is a summary of what Luke in Acts is trying to proclaim. This 'way' is what Theophilus wants to know. 'In the first part' of his work Luke 'wrote of all that Jesus did and taught from the beginning

3

until the day when, after giving instructions through the Holy Spirit to the apostles whom he had chosen, he was taken up to heaven' (1: 1–2). In the gospel the Holy Spirit had worked in Christ to establish the 'way of salvation'. In Acts the same Spirit declares through the 'servants of the Supreme God' how that 'way of salvation' should be pursued. This was 'the new way' (9: 2) whose followers Saul of Tarsus arrested and brought to Jerusalem. This was 'the way of the Lord' (18: 25) in which the Alexandrian Jew, Apollos, had been instructed. Christianity for Luke *is* 'the way of the Lord' and the Christians who journey along it are under the guidance of the Holy Spirit through the apostles. Every traveller is wise if he seeks and obtains help from those who have followed the way before. So Priscilla and Aquila took Apollos 'in hand and expounded the new way to him in greater detail' (18: 26).

On occasion the traveller will have to dissociate himself from others who fail to see clearly where the true path is leading. 'It was necessary' said Paul and Barnabas to the Jews of Pisidian Antioch, 'that the word of God should be declared to you first. But since you reject it and thus condemn yourselves as unworthy of eternal life, we now turn to the Gentiles' (13: 46). The same thing happened in Corinth. 'Your blood be on your own heads!' said Paul to the Jews, 'My conscience is clear; now I shall go to the Gentiles' (18: 6). Sometimes it is necessary to make special provisions for new companions on the journey: men and women for whom the old rules are not applicable. Thus when Paul and Barnabas, Judas and Silas 'travelled down to Antioch...and delivered the letter' (15: 30) from the apostles and elders at Jerusalem releasing Gentiles from strict conformity to the Jewish Law, 'they all rejoiced at the encouragement it brought' (15: 31).

Friendly relations with others on the way are essential if progress is to be made and most of all, wherever possible, with those in authority. Whether in Philippi, Corinth, Ephesus or Caesarea, Paul found the Roman authorities friendly, especially when his citizenship was known. The very

4

varied contacts made on the journey established the church in places as diverse as Pisidian Antioch, Philippi, Corinth, Athens and Ephesus, and its membership stretched from Africa to Rome. As its size and variety increased, so it became necessary for it to be more organized. Just as the Holy Spirit directed the way along which the Gospel should go (16: 6–10), so the seven assistants to the Twelve were selected as 'men of good reputation...full of the Spirit and of wisdom' (6: 3). In all these ways the Holy Spirit is seen at work impressing upon those who are following the way that the living Christ is truly one of their company.

'On the Sabbath they went to synagogue and took their seats' (Acts 13: 14)

This was in Pisidian Antioch, not Palestine. One of the most useful aids to the spread of the Way in the first century was the presence of a Jewish community in most towns of the Roman Empire. The larger communities possessed their synagogues, where, as at Corinth, Paul 'held discussions... Sabbath by Sabbath' (18: 4). The smaller used 'a place of prayer', which was normally 'outside the city gate by the river-side' for the convenience of ritual washing, as at Philippi (16: 13). Generally the apostles received a friendly welcome on their arrival. 'The officials of the synagogue' at Pisidian Antioch 'sent this message to them: "Friends, if you have anything to say to the people by way of exhortation, let us hear it"' (13: 15). But later 'when the Jews saw the crowds, they were filled with jealous resentment, and contradicted what Paul and Barnabas said, with violent abuse' (13: 45). The same thing happened at Thessalonica. For three Sabbaths Paul argued with the Jews in their synagogue until 'in their jealousy' they 'recruited some low fellows from the dregs of the populace, roused the rabble, and had the city in an uproar' (17: 5). At Beroea the Jews 'were more liberal-minded than those at Thessalonica' (17: 11). When Paul and Silas spoke in their synagogue 'they received the message with great eagerness' (17: 11) until the Thessalonian Jews arrived to stir up trouble. Perhaps the Jewish community in Athens was not so influential as those in other towns. Luke says little of Paul's arguments in the synagogue there and more of his discussions 'in the city square every day with casual passers-by' (17: 17).

Throughout the Roman Empire these pockets of Judaism provided Paul, the Jew and Roman citizen, with obvious bases from which to begin his mission. When, as at Corinth, opposition arose to his teaching 'that the Messiah was Jesus' (18: 5), then he left the synagogue and turned to the Gentiles, but the base had served its purpose and given him an initial hearing in the city. Judaism was an established religion in the Empire and vital to the spread of the Way. This Dispersion of the Israelites, known as the Diaspora, had begun long ago with the fall of the northern kingdom of Israel in 722 B.C. to the Assyrians and the fall of the southern kingdom of Judah in 597 B.C. to the Babylonians. The deportations that followed these defeats and other, voluntary, migrations like that to Egypt in Jeremiah 42–4 led later to the spread of Jewish communities throughout the Greek and Roman Empires. The Jewish philosopher, Philo of Alexandria (*c.* 20 B.C. to *c.* A.D. 50), tells us that in his day there were not less than a million Jews in Alexandria. These communities, despite the influence of Hellenistic culture, still paid the Temple taxes and kept the Law of Moses. They were outposts of Judaism in the Empire, to whose meetings in the synagogue Paul, 'following his usual practice', went first (17: 2). Only when the Jews had rejected his message and condemned themselves 'as unworthy of eternal life', did he say 'we now turn to the Gentiles' (13: 46).

The zeal of Jewish Christians for the Law could be a stumbling-block to the Way. When Paul made his final visit to Jerusalem and reported to James and the elders, he 'described in detail all that God had done among the Gentiles through his ministry. When they heard this, they gave praise to God' (21: 19–20). They were not so happy about the rumours that had reached them that Paul had taught 'all the Jews in the gentile world to turn their backs on Moses, telling them to give up circumcising their children and following our way of life' (21: 21). There were many thousands of Jewish converts in the city who were 'staunch upholders of the Law' (21: 20). These would have to be convinced that the rumours were false and that Paul was 'a practising Jew' and kept the Law himself (21: 24). To do this, James and the elders advised him to 'go through the ritual of purification' with four men who were under a vow and pay the expenses of their sacrifices. Such an act would prove Paul to be a practising Jew. At Cenchreae he was himself under a vow and 'had his hair cut off' (18: 18) as a sign that as a Jew he accepted the Law. The circumcision of Timothy (16: 3) is a further indication that Paul believed the Law to be binding on a Jew. Timothy was technically a Jew, as he had a Jewish mother, therefore 'out of consideration for the Jews who lived in those parts' Paul circumcised him.

The Way was a gentile mission as well as Jewish. It had been revealed to Peter at Joppa and Caesarea that 'God has no favourites' (10: 34). 'The believers who had come with Peter, men of Jewish birth, were astonished that the gift of the Holy Spirit should have been poured out even on Gentiles' (10: 45). When the church in Jerusalem heard what had happened they challenged Peter. '"You have been visiting men who are uncircumcised," they said, "and sitting at table with them!"' (11: 3). But when Peter related what had happened to him at Joppa and Caesarea, 'their doubts were silenced. They gave praise to God and said, "This means that God has granted life-giving repentance to the Gentiles also"' (11: 18). The position of the Gentiles was still not clear. Peter, Barnabas and other Jewish Christians later withdrew from meals with gentile believers at Antioch (Gal. 2: 11–13) and merited Paul's rebuke. Similarly, Jewish Christians came down from Judaea to Antioch and taught that circumcision 'in accordance with Mosaic practice' was essential to salvation (15: 1). The matter had obviously to be argued out in council. Paul, Barnabas and others from Antioch went up to Jerusalem to see the elders and apostles. The extreme Jewish view was expressed by 'some of the Pharisaic party who had become believers'. They said the Gentiles 'must be circumcised and told to keep the Law of Moses' (15: 5). After the debate James summed up. 'My judgement therefore is that we should impose no irksome restrictions on those of the Gentiles who are turning to God, but instruct them by letter to abstain from things polluted by contact with idols, from fornication, from anything that has been strangled, and from blood' (15: 19–20). These decisions were embodied in a letter to the gentile churches and handed on by Paul and his fellow-missionaries 'as they made their way from town to town' (16: 4). Although Jewish Christians were required to fulfil the Mosaic Law, there was no doubt that gentile converts were exempt. When Paul was asked to prove to the Jewish Christians in Jerusalem that he was a practising Jew, the elders repeated the decisions of the council regarding Gentiles (21: 25). The Way was consistently preached first to the Jews for whom there was no relaxation of the Mosaic Law. After that, the appeal was made to the Gentiles who, though exempt from keeping the Jewish Law, must accept the Jerusalem decrees. As time went on this distinction between Jewish and non-Jewish Christians gradually disappeared except among some Jewish Christians who tended to want to preserve it. The church soon became so independent of Judaism that the problem no longer existed.

'They also appointed elders for them in each congregation'
   (Acts 14: 23)

By the time Paul had reached the capital, the power of the Holy Spirit promised by Jesus (1: 8) had driven the church along the Roman roads throughout the Empire from Jerusalem to Rome. After the consolidation in Jerusalem following the drama of Pentecost, the number of converts increased rapidly. At the appointment of Matthias there were 'about one hundred and twenty in all' of the assembled brotherhood (1: 15). After Peter's first address 'some three thousand were added to their number' (2: 41) 'and day by day the Lord added to their number those whom he was saving' (2: 47). The total increased to 'about five thousand' men (4: 4), when Peter had addressed the crowds after the healing of the cripple at the Beautiful Gate. It was no wonder that before long the apostles would need the assistance of the Seven (6: 1–6).

The martyrdom of Stephen 'was the beginning of a time of violent persecution for the church in Jerusalem; and all except the apostles were scattered over the country districts of Judaea and Samaria' (8: 1). The next stage in the spread of Christianity had begun. Philip was at work, first in Samaria and then in the south towards Gaza. After his conversion Saul 'silenced the Jews of Damascus with his cogent proofs that Jesus was the Messiah' (9: 22). Peter's 'general tour' (9: 32) led him through Lydda to Joppa and then to Cornelius at Caesarea. 'Meanwhile those who had been scattered after the persecution that arose over Stephen made their way to Phoenicia, Cyprus, and Antioch' (11: 19). This was at first a mission to Jews only, but 'natives of Cyprus and Cyrene' among the missionaries 'began to speak to pagans as well' (11: 20). When Barnabas was sent from Jerusalem to inquire into this new movement, he rejoiced at what was happening. 'And large numbers were won over to the Lord' (11: 24). 'It was about this time' (12: 1) that Herod launched his fruitless attack on the church by killing the apostle James and imprisoning Peter. Herod died but 'the word of God continued to grow and spread' (12: 24).

The nerve-centre of the church was now at Syrian Antioch and from there the Holy Spirit sent out Barnabas and Saul, with Mark as their assistant, for work in Cyprus (13: 1–5). The subsequent journey on the mainland from Pisidian Antioch to Derbe and back is breath-taking for its speed and, despite the persecution aroused, its success. The converts now needed some form of organization. The apostles could only visit occasionally. Hardships would arise. The infant churches would need the strength of a common cause. Thus Paul and Barnabas 'appointed elders for them in each congregation, and with prayer and fasting committed them to the Lord in whom they had put their faith' (14: 23). This organization resembles that of the synagogue. The Jerusalem church was probably organized in the same way (notice the elders in 11: 30 and 15: 6). At this stage the elders or presbyters would be the senior members of the local church and formed its governing body, responsible for its worship, charity and discipline. This became the pattern for the future and its success was apparent; for when Paul and Silas revisited the towns of the Phrygian and Galatian region they found that 'day by day, the congregations grew stronger in faith and increased in numbers' (16: 5).

The meeting-place for these young churches was doubtless at first in the houses of members. Just as the church at Jerusalem met in 'the house of Mary, the mother of John Mark' (12: 12), so at Philippi it began in Lydia's house (16: 40). In Thessalonica the church may well have used Jason's house (17: 5) and in Corinth the home of Aquila and Priscilla (18: 2) or the house of Titius Justus 'next door to the synagogue' (18: 7). Paul's repeated journeys over the same territory brought 'new strength to all the converts' (18: 23) of these new and growing churches.

Contacts between local churches were established. Priscilla and Aquila, now in Ephesus, gave hospitality to Apollos and then, 'finding that he wished to go across to Achaia, the brotherhood gave him their support, and wrote to the congregation there to make him welcome' (18: 27). Discussions not only took place in synagogues but also in pagan lecture-halls like that of Tyrannus in Ephesus (19: 9), or before the Court of Areopagus, probably in the colonnade surrounding the market-place in Athens (17: 19–23). On his last journey

back to Jerusalem Paul conducted worship in a room on the
third floor of a house in Troas (20: 8–9) and gave his final
charge to the elders of Ephesus at Miletus. 'Keep watch over
yourselves and over all the flock of which the Holy Spirit has
given you charge, as shepherds of the church of the Lord,
which he won for himself by his own blood' (20: 28). For
three years Paul had trained them (20: 31); now they must be
left to themselves. The church was to be found everywhere
along Paul's route—at Tyre and Ptolemais, at Caesarea and
back in Jerusalem. Paul's task was nearly accomplished. He
had fulfilled the Lord's commission given through Ananias:
'this man is my chosen instrument to bring my name before
the nations and their kings, and before the people of Israel'
(9: 15). Now the Lord appeared to him while under arrest
in Jerusalem, 'and said, "Keep up your courage; you have
affirmed the truth about me in Jerusalem, and you must do
the same in Rome"' (23: 11). The same assurances were given
on the stormy voyage across the Mediterranean. '"Do not
be afraid, Paul," he said; "it is ordained that you shall appear
before the Emperor"' (27: 24). When the winter was passed,
the final stage of the voyage was completed and Paul reached
Rome. The church had been established throughout the Empire and was ready to conquer the capital itself.

'Proclaiming the kingdom of God and teaching the facts about the Lord Jesus Christ' (Acts 28: 31)

This is what Paul did during the two years he spent in
Rome, but the whole of Acts is doing precisely the same for
all time. The book is a conversation piece. To look with
scholarly precision for the sources of Acts is rather like trying
to track down the lines of argument in a discussion round a
dinner-table to their original contributors. It is impossible.
In his Gospel Luke told Theophilus that in his turn he had
followed 'the traditions handed down to us by the original
eyewitnesses and servants of the Gospel' (Luke 1: 2). He

clearly did the same in Acts. Some of these traditions were doubtless found in written records (e.g. the 'we-sections'), but the majority must have been the contributions of friend to friend along the way—some at first hand but many more the outcome of memories or reminiscence.

Barnabas may well have been a key figure in those early days, watching with keen insight the work of the apostles before he sold his field and 'brought the money, and laid it at the apostles' feet' (4: 37). It would be easy for Barnabas to recall the stories and the very words of Peter and John. Mark too must well have remembered the prayer meetings at his mother's house and the occasion when one meeting was disturbed by a knocking at the door which the maid was too overjoyed to open (12: 14). Timothy, Silas, James and Paul himself must have told their tales. The conversion of Cornelius must have been discussed over and over again. This was a new departure along the way. Did it lead to a dead end or was it a new turning with more ahead? The story of Cornelius and his friends is a reminder of the astonishing fact that 'the gift of the Holy Spirit should have been poured out even on Gentiles' (10: 45). Paul's stay in Corinth is full of these contacts that are the realities of life and thus the stuff of the Christian way. 'He fell in with a Jew named Aquila, a native of Pontus, and his wife Priscilla...and, because he was of the same trade, he made his home with them, and they carried on business together; they were tent-makers' (18: 2–3). This was an obvious thing to do: they had common interests. And the Christian way followed. In one sense Acts is not a scholar's book to dig and probe and select. It is a book of vital contacts and lively recollections that Luke has culled from friends and acquaintances and with consummate skill has ordered and written down. Through these anecdotes and reminiscences, through these signs of his presence the Holy Spirit leads the Christian along the way of true discipleship. Luke was the first to study closely the traditions of the church and so to begin the writing of its history.

There can be no certainty of the date when Acts was written. The final events recorded must have taken place in the very early sixties. If Luke's Gospel was written, as most scholars suggest, between A.D. 75 and 85 then it seems probable that Acts followed in the late eighties. There have been arguments for an earlier date, even that Acts was written before Luke. For example, the book contains no reference to Paul's later years and death. There is no link between the story of Paul in Acts and the journeyings revealed in his letters. This suggests that his letters were not yet in widespread circulation. Indeed the conversion story in Galatians 1: 13–24 differs considerably from the three accounts in Acts (9: 1–30; 22: 1–21; 26: 4–18). Acts says nothing of Nero's persecution nor of the fall of Jerusalem in A.D. 70.

On the other hand, the differences between Acts and Paul's letters could indicate that Acts was written much later. The memory plays tricks, especially when the details of an event are handed on by word of mouth.

Some scholars find proof for a late date for Acts in Gamaliel's speech (5: 36–7). There Gamaliel refers to the rebellions of Theudas (A.D. 44–5) and Judas the Galilean (A.D. 6) and seems to get them in the wrong chronological order. This mistake is said to be owing to Luke's misreading of Josephus' book *The Antiquities of the Jews*, which was published about A.D. 94. If this be so, then Luke must have written Acts late in the first century. But if Luke is quoting Gamaliel correctly, the reference must be to another rebellion of Theudas than that known to Josephus (see below, pp. 47–8). It need not argue a late date for Acts.

The absence of any direct reference in Acts to Paul's well-known collection for the poor in Jerusalem (1 Cor. 16: 1) might be stronger evidence for a late date. It would then indicate that, when Luke wrote, the emergency was long past.

'*Day by day the Lord added to their number those whom he was saving*' (Acts 2: 47)

And that is what Acts is about. In his commentary on Luke's Gospel in this series, E. J. Tinsley writes: 'In the Gospel the Spirit comes with Christ, in Acts Christ comes with the Spirit. It is the one coming of the one God who always comes the same way—by "signs"!' (p. 213). Acts, then, is the account of a Holy War. The Spirit had come with 'power' (1: 8) as Christ promised. These are 'the last days' of which the prophet spoke (Joel 2: 28–32; Acts 2: 14–21). 'Yes, I will endue even my slaves, both men and women, with a portion of my spirit, and they shall prophesy' (2: 18). This was not some placid, historical tale, that Luke was describing. It was a divine revolution which did not stop at rich or poor, Jew or Gentile, man or woman. The Lord in the Spirit was out to save and this is how he did it.

Of course the book indicates the Christian insistence on the moral law, the gradual growth of organization in the church, the establishment of an agreed doctrine; but these are subsidiary to the central theme that 'day by day the Lord added to their number those whom he was saving' (2: 47). 'One day at three in the afternoon' (3: 1) it was a cripple at the Beautiful Gate. On another, during a journey to the south, it 'was a eunuch, a high official of the Kandake, or Queen, of Ethiopia, in charge of all her treasure' (8: 27). It would not all be easy going. A war never is. So the Spirit, through Ananias, said of Saul, one of his greatest captives: 'I myself will show him all that he must go through for my name's sake' (9: 16). When the Spirit had 'Cornelius, a centurion in the Italian Cohort' (10: 1) at Caesarea in mind, 'next day... about noon' he acted upon Peter. 'Some men are here looking for you; make haste and go downstairs' (10: 9, 19). The Spirit, through Paul, argued 'in the city square every day with casual passers-by' (17: 17), or, through Priscilla and Aquila, in the privacy of their home, took the learned Apollos 'in hand and expounded the new way to him in greater detail' (18: 26). One of the dangers a commentary inflicts upon a reader is a too great concern for detailed exposition. In the succeeding pages, when comment is being made on a particular verse, the *action* of the whole book must never be forgotten; Acts is about men and women and the Holy Spirit capturing them as slaves for Christ. 'This much I will admit:' said Paul to the Governor Felix, 'I am a follower of the new way...and it is in that manner that I worship the God of our fathers' (24: 14).

THE PLAN OF ACTS

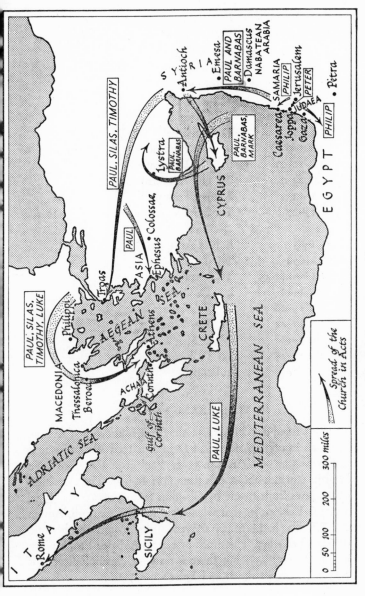

The Mediterranean world in Acts

17

A TIME-CHART FOR ACTS

The only fixed date in Acts is Gallio's proconsulship of Achaia. From an inscription found at Delphi in 1905 we know that Gallio was in office in A.D. 51–2. Paul must therefore have been in Corinth about this time (18: 12–17). The expulsion of the Jews from Rome by Claudius (18: 2) was probably in A.D. 49. Luke notes that when Paul reached Corinth, Aquila and Priscilla 'had recently arrived' there 'from Italy' because of Claudius' edict. The death of Herod Agrippa I took place in A.D. 44 (12: 23); but there is no clear chronological link between Herod's death and Peter's imprisonment, or Paul's first journey, which Luke describes before and after it. Similarly, the date of the famine in the reign of Claudius (A.D. 41–54) and the date of Agabus' prophecy about it (11: 28) are not evident from the text. The period of Sergius Paulus' proconsulship in Cyprus is not known (13: 7) and, thus, the time of Paul's visit to him is uncertain. Even the year when Porcius Festus succeeded Felix (25: 1) cannot be determined accurately, though *c.* A.D 59 is a possible date.

A tentative time-chart might be as follows:

A.D.		Acts
30	Ascension of Jesus	1: 6–11
	Appointment of the Seven	6: 1–7
	Death of Stephen	7: 54 — 8: 1*a*
35	Conversion of Saul	9: 1–30
40	Church in Antioch	11: 19–30
	Execution of James and Imprisonment of Peter	12: 1–25
45	Paul's first journey	13: 1 — 14: 28
	? Galatians	
	Council at Jerusalem	15: 1–35
50	Paul's second journey	15: 36 — 18: 22
	1 Thessalonians, 2 Thessalonians	
	Paul's third journey	18: 23 — 21: 17

| 55 | — | ? *Galatians*, 1 *Corinthians*, *Romans*, |
| | | 2 *Corinthians* and ? *Philippians* |

| | | Paul's arrest in Jerusalem | 21: 27–36 |

60	—	Paul's journey to Rome	27: 1 — 28: 15
		Two full years in Rome	28: 30–1
		Colossians, Philemon, ? Ephesians and ? *Philippians*
		Mark
		? Paul's journey to Spain, Ephesus, Macedonia and
65	—	Greece
		? 1 *Timothy*, *Titus*, 2 *Timothy* or much later
		Death of Peter and Paul

| 70 | — |

| 75 | — | *Luke–Acts* (see pp. 12–13) |

✳   ✳   ✳   ✳   ✳   ✳   ✳   ✳   ✳   ✳   ✳   ✳   ✳

The Beginnings of the Church

THE AUTHOR'S PREFACE

1 IN THE FIRST PART of my work, Theophilus, I wrote
2 of all that Jesus did and taught from the beginning until
the day when, after giving instructions through the Holy
Spirit to the apostles whom he had chosen, he was taken
3 up to heaven. He showed himself to these men after his
death, and gave ample proof that he was alive: over a

period of forty days he appeared to them and taught them about the kingdom of God. While he was in their com- 4 pany he told them not to leave Jerusalem. 'You must wait', he said, 'for the promise made by my Father, about which you have heard me speak: John, as you know, 5 baptized with water, but you will be baptized with the Holy Spirit, and within the next few days.'

✵ The author clearly intends his work to be read as a whole. Part 1 was the Gospel. Part 2 is now to follow on from the final earthly appearance of Jesus at his Ascension. Jesus gives his last instruction *You must wait...for the promise made by my Father* (1: 4), that is, the gift of the Holy Spirit.

1. Like the Gospel (Luke 1: 1), Acts is addressed to *Theophilus*. In Luke 1: 3 he is given the title 'your Excellency' which is used in Acts only for the Roman Governors Felix and Festus (23: 26; 24: 2; 26: 25). The Greek name means 'a friend of God'. Is the work therefore addressed to any friend of God, i.e. the reader, or is Theophilus the pseudonym for some leading Roman in government service who wanted to be persuaded about the Way before committing himself openly to following it? Whoever he was in reality, he is certainly representative of the long line of God's friends of whom we shall hear as the story unfolds.

3. The purpose of the post-resurrection appearances was to prove that Jesus *was alive*. The apostles were instructed to wait in Jerusalem, from where the Holy Spirit would send them out. ✵

JESUS' FAREWELL

So, when they were all together, they asked him, 'Lord, 6 is this the time when you are to establish once again the sovereignty of Israel?' He answered, 'It is not for you 7 to know about dates or times, which the Father has set

8 within his own control. But you will receive power when
the Holy Spirit comes upon you; and you will bear witness for me in Jerusalem, and all over Judaea and Samaria,
and away to the ends of the earth.'

9   When he had said this, as they watched, he was lifted
10 up, and a cloud removed him from their sight. As he was
going, and as they were gazing intently into the sky, all
11 at once there stood beside them two men in white who
said, 'Men of Galilee, why stand there looking up into
the sky? This Jesus, who has been taken away from you
up to heaven, will come in the same way as you have
seen him go.'

* The Ascension in Acts expands the brief reference in the
Third Gospel (24: 50–3) and thereby emphasizes the con-
tinuity, not only of the two books, but of the work of Christ
in the Gospel and of its continuation through the Spirit in
Acts. This is in no sense the end of the mission. *This Jesus...
will come in the same way as you have seen him go.*

6–8. The question still gives the impression that the apostles
did not fully understand the nature of Christ's kingdom,
though it need not indicate that they were thinking only in
terms of an earthly empire. Whatever they had in mind, Jesus
makes it clear in his answer (1) that dates and times are
irrelevant and the Father's business not theirs; (2) that the
Holy Spirit will fill them with power for the work to be done;
they will not go unaided; (3) that all the world is their mission-
field, beginning at home in Jerusalem. Acts itself is planned
on this outward-reaching scheme.

9–11. Too much emphasis must not be placed on the
physical event known as the Ascension. Comparisons with
similar Old Testament happenings, e.g. Enoch (Gen. 5: 24);
Elijah (2 Kings 2: 11), suggest that the same kind of picture
is being used, indicating in each case a conception of the world

different from our own knowledge of it. Perhaps the best comparison is with the Transfiguration (Luke 9: 28–36). The Ascension is in a sense a final Transfiguration. Henceforth Jesus is one with the Father. It is also a completion of the Resurrection and is so symbolized by the two heavenly witnesses (cf. Luke 24: 4). The cloud is more like the dropping of the curtain at the end of Scene I than an indication of the divine presence (cf. Exod. 19: 9).   *

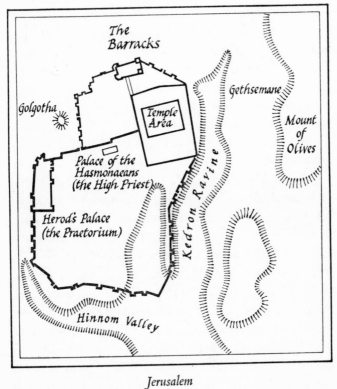

Jerusalem

THE COMPANY IN JERUSALEM

12 Then they returned to Jerusalem from the hill called Olivet, which is near Jerusalem, no farther than a Sab-
13 bath day's journey. Entering the city they went to the room upstairs where they were lodging: Peter and John and James and Andrew, Philip and Thomas, Bartholomew and Matthew, James son of Alphaeus and Simon the
14 Zealot, and Judas son of James. All these were constantly at prayer together, and with them a group of women, including Mary the mother of Jesus, and his brothers.

15 It was during this time that Peter stood up before the assembled brotherhood, about one hundred and twenty
16 in all, and said: 'My friends, the prophecy in Scripture was bound to come true, which the Holy Spirit, through the mouth of David, uttered about Judas who acted as
17 guide to those who arrested Jesus. For he was one of our
18 number and had his place in this ministry.' (This Judas, be it noted, after buying a plot of land with the price of his villainy, fell forward on the ground, and burst open,
19 so that his entrails poured out. This became known to everyone in Jerusalem, and they named the property in their own language Akeldama, which means 'Blood
20 Acre'.) 'The text I have in mind', Peter continued, 'is in the Book of Psalms: "Let his homestead fall desolate; let there be none to inhabit it"; and again, "Let another take
21 over his charge." Therefore one of those who bore us company all the while we had the Lord Jesus with us,
22 coming and going, from John's ministry of baptism until the day when he was taken up from us—one of those must now join us as a witness to his resurrection.'

24

Two names were put forward: Joseph, who was known 23
as Barsabbas, and bore the added name of Justus; and
Matthias. Then they prayed and said, 'Thou, Lord, who 24
knowest the hearts of all men, declare which of these two
thou hast chosen to receive this office of ministry and 25
apostleship which Judas abandoned to go where he belonged.' They drew lots and the lot fell on Matthias, who 26
was then assigned a place among the twelve apostles.

✻ When the party returned the short distance from Olivet
to Jerusalem, it almost seems as if Peter checks the register:
the Twelve, the women, Jesus' mother, his brothers and so on
—*about one hundred and twenty in all*, with one significant
absentee from the list. The order of the apostles is slightly
different from that in Luke 6: 14–16. The place where they
met—*the room upstairs where they were lodging*—may well have
been the scene of the Last Supper and probably in the house
of Mary the mother of John Mark (12: 12).

14. As is usual in Luke, prayer precedes a great event; cf. the
night before the appointment of the Twelve which was spent
by Jesus in prayer (Luke 6: 12).

15–20. Peter takes the lead immediately. The quotations
from Psalms 69: 25 and 109: 8 for Judas' defection are typical
of early Christian witnesses, seeking to 'prove' to their fellow
Jews that Jesus was the Messiah by showing that all the events
connected with him were foretold in the Old Testament.

18–19. The story of Judas' death differs from that in Matt.
27: 3–10, where he hanged himself. The chief priests took up
the money which he had thrown back and bought 'the Potter's
Field, as a burial-place for foreigners'. Luke obviously adds
the explanation in Acts for the information of his readers and
translates the Aramaic *Akeldama* as Field of Blood or *Blood
Acre*. Luke's tradition of Judas' death is a very different one
from Matthew's but both reflect the belief of the early church
that the traitor came to a horrible end. It is possible that the

2-2

dead body hanging from a tree was torn down and ripped open by wild dogs, thus suggesting both traditions.

21–2. The qualification for apostleship was to have been an associate of Jesus from his baptism to his ascension. The work of an apostle was to be *a witness to his resurrection*.

23–6. Once again Luke notes the prayer before an important event; this time the appointment of Matthias to make up the number of apostles to twelve, like the twelve patriarchs of the old Israel. Some authorities read Barnabas for Barsabbas. A Judas Barsabbas accompanied Paul, Barnabas and Silas from the council at Jerusalem to Antioch (15: 22).   ✴

THE HOLY SPIRIT AT PENTECOST

2 While the day of Pentecost was running its course they
2 were all together in one place, when suddenly there came from the sky a noise like that of a strong driving wind, which filled the whole house where they were sitting.
3 And there appeared to them tongues like flames of fire,
4 dispersed among them and resting on each one. And they were all filled with the Holy Spirit and began to talk in other tongues, as the Spirit gave them power of utterance.
5 Now there were living in Jerusalem devout Jews drawn
6 from every nation under heaven; and at this sound the crowd gathered, all bewildered because each one heard
7 the apostles talking in his own language. They were amazed and in their astonishment exclaimed, 'Why, they are all Galileans, are they not, these men who are speaking?
8 How is it then that we hear them, each of us in his own
9 native language? Parthians, Medes, Elamites; inhabitants of Mesopotamia, of Judaea and Cappadocia, of Pontus
10 and Asia, of Phrygia and Pamphylia, of Egypt and the districts of Libya around Cyrene; visitors from Rome,

both Jews and proselytes, Cretans and Arabs, we hear 11
them telling in our own tongues the great things God has
done.' And they were all amazed and perplexed, saying 12
to one another, 'What can this mean?' Others said con- 13
temptuously, 'They have been drinking!'

---

* The harvest festival, celebrated fifty (Greek *pentekonta*) days
after Passover and also known as the Feast of Weeks (Lev.
23: 15–21), had come to be a commemoration of the gift of
the Law as well. Hence its appropriateness for the gift of the
Spirit is apparent in the accompanying *noise like that of a strong
driving wind* and *tongues like flames of fire*. (Exod. 19: 18–19,
'the Lord descended...in fire: and...the voice of the trumpet
waxed louder and louder'. Cf. Elijah's experience on Horeb in
1 Kings 19: 11–14.) The event, whatever its actual form, was
ominous for the future—the wind of the Spirit breathed power
into all those gathered there (cf. 'the breath of life', Gen. 2: 7;
Jesus 'breathed on them, saying, "Receive the Holy Spirit!"'
John 20: 22); the fire cleansed and illumined their minds (cf.
Matt. 3: 11, 'he will baptize you with the Holy Spirit and with
fire'); and the gift of tongues (*glossolalia*) was symbolic of
the world-wide work they were to do (1: 8).

5–13. Clearly the pilgrims in the city believed that the
apostles were *telling in our own tongues the great things God has
done*, but equally clearly much must have been incomprehen-
sible, for *others said contemptuously, 'They have been drinking!'*
No doubt belief and scepticism were both aroused at what
was heard. Ecstatic utterance was certainly part of the stock-
in-trade of the early church but its value was doubted by some
(e.g. Paul in 1 Cor. 14: 19, 'in the congregation I would rather
speak five intelligible words, for the benefit of others as well
as myself, than thousands of words in the language of ecstasy').

5. Some manuscripts omit *Jews* but this would indicate
that the Gentile mission began right from the first, which is
not likely.

27

8–11. Attempts have been made to find some order in the list of nations, with little success. The most impressive is that based on astrological geography, whereby each country is allotted to one of the signs of the Zodiac, as in the list drawn up by Paul of Alexandria in A.D. 378. Luke begins in Parthia in the east and proceeds as far west as the province of Asia. He then doubles back round the Levant to North Africa. Judaea is oddly out of place and in the summing up at the end *Cretans and Arabs* might mean 'all, from the isles to the deserts'. The peoples named indicate the world-wide nature of the Dispersion (see p. 6)—Jews scattered throughout the Middle East. ✶

PETER SPEAKS TO THE CROWD

14 But Peter stood up with the Eleven, raised his voice, and addressed them: 'Fellow Jews, and all you who live in
15 Jerusalem, mark this and give me a hearing. These men are not drunk, as you imagine; for it is only nine in the
16,17 morning. No, this is what the prophet spoke of: "God says, 'This will happen in the last days: I will pour out upon everyone a portion of my spirit; and your sons and daughters shall prophesy; your young men shall see
18 visions, and your old men shall dream dreams. Yes, I will endue even my slaves, both men and women, with a
19 portion of my spirit, and they shall prophesy. And I will show portents in the sky above, and signs on the earth
20 below—blood and fire and drifting smoke. The sun shall be turned to darkness, and the moon to blood, before that great, resplendent day, the day of the Lord, shall come.
21 And then, everyone who invokes the name of the Lord shall be saved.'"

22   'Men of Israel, listen to me: I speak of Jesus of Nazareth,

a man singled out by God and made known to you through miracles, portents, and signs, which God worked among you through him, as you well know. When he 23 had been given up to you, by the deliberate will and plan of God, you used heathen men to crucify and kill him. But God raised him to life again, setting him free from 24 the pangs of death, because it could not be that death should keep him in its grip.

'For David says of him: 25

"I foresaw that the presence of the Lord would be with
        me always,
  For he is at my right hand so that I may not be shaken;
  Therefore my heart was glad and my tongue spoke 26
        my joy;
  Moreover, my flesh shall dwell in hope,
  For thou wilt not abandon my soul to Hades,   27
  Nor let thy loyal servant suffer corruption.
  Thou hast shown me the ways of life,   28
  Thou wilt fill me with gladness by thy presence."

'Let me tell you plainly, my friends, that the patriarch 29 David died and was buried, and his tomb is here to this very day. It is clear therefore that he spoke as a prophet 30 who knew that God had sworn to him that one of his own direct descendants should sit on his throne; and when 31 he said he was not abandoned to Hades, and his flesh never suffered corruption, he spoke with foreknowledge of the resurrection of the Messiah. The Jesus we speak of has 32 been raised by God, as we can all bear witness. Exalted 33 thus with God's right hand, he received the Holy Spirit from the Father, as was promised, and all that you now

34 see and hear flows from him. For it was not David who
   went up to heaven; his own words are: "The Lord said
35 to my Lord, 'Sit at my right hand until I make your
36 enemies your footstool.'" Let all Israel then accept as
   certain that God has made this Jesus, whom you crucified,
   both Lord and Messiah.'

✶ The best evidence of the power of the Spirit given at
Pentecost is in Peter's speech, if his fearlessness before the
crowd is compared with his denial of Christ before the crucifixion (Luke 22: 54–61). The speech itself contains the
following points which are the basis for Peter's faith and the
foundation on which the church was built:

(1) The ecstasy was not the result of drunkenness (it was
only 9 a.m.!). It was the outpouring of God's spirit as prophesied by Joel (2: 28–32).

(2) Jesus, who was approved by his mighty works among
them, had been crucified and raised up according to God's
plan.

(3) *The pangs of death* could not restrain Jesus the Messiah,
as David in the Psalms (16: 8–11) had prophesied.

(4) David knew that his descendant would be the Messiah
(Ps. 110: 1). This Messiah is Jesus.

(5) We are witnesses to this fact through his resurrection.

(6) *All that you now see and hear flows from him* through the
Holy Spirit.

(7) *God has made this Jesus, whom you crucified, both Lord
and Messiah.*

There is no doubt that, in common with other speeches in
Acts (e.g. Stephen's, 7: 1–53; Paul's, 13: 16–41), this one of
Peter's is Luke's *composition*. But, like the others, it is not his
invention. The speeches in Acts have often been compared
with those in Thucydides' writings, and the method of both
historians would seem to be the same. Neither claimed to
produce the exact words spoken but both reported as nearly

as possible the substance of the speakers' words, using as a basis what they had heard themselves or what had been reported to them by others who had heard the speeches delivered.

16. The N.E.B., following some manuscripts, omits the prophet's name—Joel.

17–21. The prophecy refers to God present in power through the Spirit (cf. the gift of the Spirit to the seventy elders of Israel and to Eldad and Medad, Num. 11: 23–9, 'would God that all the Lord's people were prophets, that the Lord would put his spirit upon them!' (verse 29)). The quotation is largely from the Septuagint (LXX), the Greek version of the Old Testament.

25–8. Ps. 16: 8–11 again from LXX. *

WHAT HAPPENED AFTERWARDS

When they heard this they were cut to the heart, and said 37 to Peter and the apostles, 'Friends, what are we to do?' 'Repent,' said Peter, 'repent and be baptized, every one 38 of you, in the name of Jesus the Messiah for the forgiveness of your sins; and you will receive the gift of the Holy Spirit. For the promise is to you, and to your children, 39 and to all who are far away, everyone whom the Lord our God may call.'

In these and many other words he pressed his case and 40 pleaded with them: 'Save yourselves', he said, 'from this crooked age.' Then those who accepted his word were 41 baptized, and some three thousand were added to their number that day.

They met constantly to hear the apostles teach, and 42 to share the common life, to break bread, and to pray. A sense of awe was everywhere, and many marvels and 43

44 signs were brought about through the apostles. All whose
faith had drawn them together held everything in com-
45 mon: they would sell their property and possessions and
make a general distribution as the need of each required.
46 With one mind they kept up their daily attendance at the
temple, and, breaking bread in private houses, shared
47 their meals with unaffected joy, as they praised God and
enjoyed the favour of the whole people. And day by day
the Lord added to their number those whom he was
saving.

✶ The effects of Peter's speech were dramatic and far-reaching:

(1) Many were *cut to the heart* and asked the apostles:
Friends, what are we to do?

(2) Peter told them to *repent and be baptized...in the name
of Jesus the Messiah*. They would then *receive the gift of the Holy
Spirit*. Baptism had a new significance, since it was now *in the
name of Jesus*, i.e. into his ownership so that he could work
in them through his Spirit.

(3) *Some three thousand were added to their number.*

(4) Christian worship began to take shape, with the
teaching, the common life or fellowship, the breaking of
bread, and prayers.

(5) The Spirit worked signs and wonders through the
apostles, as evidence of the new age.

(6) Believers held their possessions in common.

(7) They sold their property and gave to the poor.

(8) They continued to worship in the Temple (i.e. they
continued to exercise their rights of worship as Jews), but they
broke bread *in private houses* or 'from house to house'.

(9) The church grew daily.

42–7. The picture of the early church is one of amazed
wonder, common fellowship and *unaffected joy*, in *the favour
of the whole people* (if not of their rulers!). ✶

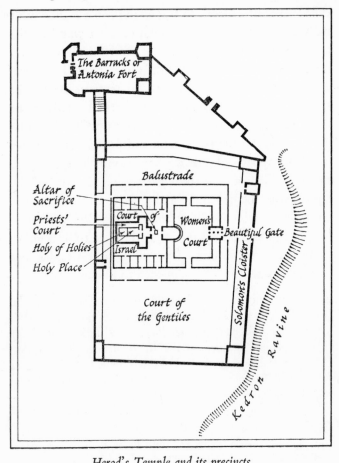

The Barracks or
Antonia Fort

Balustrade

Altar of
Sacrifice

Priests'
Court

Holy of Holies

Holy Place

Court of
Israel

Court of

Women's

Court

Beautiful Gate

Solomon's Cloister

Court of
the Gentiles

Kedron Ravine

Herod's Temple and its precincts

AT THE BEAUTIFUL GATE

One day at three in the afternoon, the hour of prayer, **3**
Peter and John were on their way up to the temple. Now ₂
a man who had been a cripple from birth used to be
carried there and laid every day by the gate of the temple

called 'Beautiful Gate', to beg from people as they went
3 in. When he saw Peter and John on their way into the
4 temple he asked for charity. But Peter fixed his eyes on
5 him, as John did also, and said, 'Look at us.' Expecting
6 a gift from them, the man was all attention. And Peter
said, 'I have no silver or gold; but what I have I give you:
7 in the name of Jesus Christ of Nazareth, walk.' Then he
grasped him by the right hand and pulled him up; and
8 at once his feet and ankles grew strong; he sprang up,
stood on his feet, and started to walk. He entered the
temple with them, leaping and praising God as he went.
9, 10 Everyone saw him walking and praising God, and when
they recognized him as the man who used to sit begging
at Beautiful Gate, they were filled with wonder and
amazement at what had happened to him.

* Luke at once, almost abruptly, illustrates by one of the
'many marvels and signs' (2: 43) that the new age had dawned.
The time and place are precise—*three in the afternoon*, the hour
of the evening sacrifice, at the *Beautiful Gate*. The healing
closely resembles that by Paul of the 'crippled man' at Lystra
(14: 8–10). The witnesses are exactly stated. *Everyone*, in the
temple, *saw him walking and praising God.*

2. *Beautiful Gate*: probably that linking the Court of the
Gentiles with the Court of the Women.

3. John is closely associated with Peter in these early days.

6. As with baptism (2: 38), so with healing, it was *in the
name of Jesus Christ.* *

THE MEANING OF THE SIGN

11 And as he was clutching Peter and John all the people
came running in astonishment towards them in Solomon's
12 Cloister, as it is called. Peter saw them coming and met

them with these words: 'Men of Israel, why be surprised at this? Why stare at us as if we had made this man walk by some power or godliness of our own? The God of 13 Abraham, Isaac, and Jacob, the God of our fathers, has given the highest honour to his servant Jesus, whom you committed for trial and repudiated in Pilate's court—repudiated the one who was holy and righteous when 14 Pilate had decided to release him. You begged as a favour the release of a murderer, and killed him who has led the 15 way to life. But God raised him from the dead; of that we are witnesses. And the name of Jesus, by awakening 16 faith, has strengthened this man, whom you see and know, and this faith has made him completely well, as you can all see for yourselves.

'And now, my friends, I know quite well that you 17 acted in ignorance, and so did your rulers; but this is how 18 God fulfilled what he had foretold in the utterances of all the prophets: that his Messiah should suffer. Repent then 19 and turn to God, so that your sins may be wiped out. Then the Lord may grant you a time of recovery and 20 send you the Messiah he has already appointed, that is, Jesus. He must be received into heaven until the time of 21 universal restoration comes, of which God spoke by his holy prophets. Moses said, "The Lord God will raise up 22 a prophet for you from among yourselves as he raised me; you shall listen to everything he says to you, and 23 anyone who refuses to listen to that prophet must be extirpated from Israel." And so said all the prophets, from 24 Samuel onwards; with one voice they all predicted this present time.

'You are the heirs of the prophets; you are within 25

35

The Beginnings of the Church

the covenant which God made with your fathers, when he said to Abraham, "And in your offspring all the 26 families on earth shall find blessing." When God raised up his Servant, he sent him to you first, to bring you blessing by turning every one of you from your wicked ways.'

✵ In Solomon's Cloister or portico, probably opposite the Beautiful Gate on the east side of the temple area, Peter and John were surrounded by the astonished crowd. Peter, with the same technique as in his earlier speech, uses his opportunity to assert that *the name of Jesus, by awakening faith, has strengthened this man*. The whole blame for the death of Jesus is thrust upon his hearers, *but God raised him from the dead; of that we are witnesses*. This is the way in which *God fulfilled what he had foretold in the utterances of all the prophets*. Despite Peter's emphasis on Jewish responsibility for the death of Jesus, it must be remembered that the real authority was with Rome. Pressures in the early church led to an emphasis on Roman recognition of Christianity and the antagonism between Jews and Christians. Some Jewish leaders—even priests (6: 7)— became members of the new community.

14. Luke had emphasized in his Gospel that Pilate had acquitted Jesus (Luke 23: 13–25).

13–18. The list of titles given to Jesus impresses upon the crowd the messianic nature of his mission—*his* (God's) *servant Jesus*; ...*one who was holy and righteous*; ...*him who has led the way to life*; ...*his Messiah*.

21. *the time of universal restoration*: the time when God's purpose for the world will be realized and a new life established.

22–3. The quotation is a combination of texts: Deut. 18: 15, 18, 19; Lev. 23: 29. Cf. Stephen's use of the same reference (7: 37).

24. Omitting Moses, Samuel is the first prophet (1 Sam.

3: 20) and from him onwards, prophets had looked for the
coming of the messianic age.

25–6. The blessing promised by God to Abraham (Gen.
22: 18) is fulfilled in Jesus. ✶

A SKIRMISH WITH THE RULERS

They were still addressing the people when the chief **4**
priests came upon them, together with the Controller of
the Temple and the Sadducees, exasperated at their 2
teaching the people and proclaiming the resurrection from
the dead—the resurrection of Jesus. They were arrested 3
and put in prison for the night, as it was already evening.
But many of those who had heard the message became 4
believers. The number of men now reached about five
thousand.

Next day the Jewish rulers, elders, and doctors of the 5
law met in Jerusalem. There were present Annas the High 6
Priest, Caiaphas, Jonathan, Alexander, and all who were
of the high-priestly family. They brought the apostles 7
before the court and began the examination. 'By what
power', they asked, 'or by what name have such men as
you done this?' Then Peter, filled with the Holy Spirit, 8
answered, 'Rulers of the people and elders, if the question 9
put to us today is about help given to a sick man, and we
are asked by what means he was cured, here is the answer, 10
for all of you and for all the people of Israel: it was by
the name of Jesus Christ of Nazareth, whom you crucified,
whom God raised from the dead; it is by his name that
this man stands here before you fit and well. This Jesus 11
is the stone rejected by the builders which has become the
keystone—and you are the builders. There is no salvation 12

in anyone else at all, for there is no other name under heaven granted to men, by which we may receive salvation.'

13 Now as they observed the boldness of Peter and John, and noted that they were untrained laymen, they began to wonder, then recognized them as former companions 14 of Jesus. And when they saw the man who had been cured standing with them, they had nothing to say in 15 reply. So they ordered them to leave the court, and then 16 discussed the matter among themselves. 'What are we to do with these men?' they said; 'for it is common knowledge in Jerusalem that a notable miracle has come 17 about through them; and we cannot deny it. But to stop this from spreading further among the people, we had better caution them never again to speak to anyone in 18 this name.' They then called them in and ordered them to refrain from all public speaking and teaching in the name of Jesus.

19 But Peter and John said to them in reply: 'Is it right in God's eyes for us to obey you rather than God? Judge for 20 yourselves. We cannot possibly give up speaking of things we have seen and heard.'

21 The court repeated the caution and discharged them. They could not see how they were to punish them, because the people were all giving glory to God for what 22 had happened. The man upon whom this miracle of healing had been performed was over forty years old.

* The teaching of Peter and John was stirring up popular enthusiasm: *many of those who had heard the message became believers. The number of men now reached about five thousand.* The rulers became actively hostile. The *priests* (some manuscripts omit *chief*) were those in charge of temple worship. The *Controller of the Temple* was probably second in command to the High Priest and in charge of order in the Temple. The *Sadducees*, who probably had this name because they claimed to be descended from Zadok the priest of David's time (2 Sam. 8: 17), but who became a party during the Maccabaean period (second century B.C.), opposed the apostles on both religious and political grounds. They adhered strictly to the written law and rejected the Pharisees' attempt to apply it to the changing aspects of life. In particular, the Sadducees denied 'that there is any resurrection, or angel, or spirit, but the Pharisees accept them' (23: 8). Cf. Luke 20: 27–38, where the Sadducees argue with Jesus. They feared for their own position if the apostles' preaching brought about Roman interference.

3. The persecution foretold by Jesus begins (Luke 12: 11–12; 21: 12–19).

5. The effect of Peter's speech was to bring together the Sanhedrin or Supreme Court consisting of the priests and the elders or members of the leading families, who were largely Sadducees, and the doctors of the law, who were mostly Pharisees.

6. *Annas* was *High Priest* from A.D. 6 to A.D. 15 but remained influential during the reign of his son-in-law, *Caiaphas*, A.D. c. 18–36. *Jonathan* (or John in some manuscripts) is probably Caiaphas' successor. *Alexander* is not known.

Luke continues to people his stage with a fascinating group. The learned Sanhedrin is set against the *untrained laymen* whom they recognized *as former companions of Jesus*, and *they had nothing to say in reply*. The action pauses in a dramatic tableau. The sick man cured and standing in the midst was the sign of Christ's presence through the Holy Spirit. *Here is the answer, for all of you and for all the people of Israel: it was by the name of Jesus Christ of Nazareth, whom you crucified, whom God raised from the dead* (verse 10). This was the message the apostles were commissioned to proclaim and no amount of official majesty could restrain them (verses 19–20).

The Beginnings of the Church

The end of this incident was a discharge with a warning.

11. The text is from Ps. 118: 22 and was used by Jesus himself (Luke 20: 17). Further use of this reference is in 1 Pet. 2: 7. *The stone rejected by the builders* had mysteriously become *the keystone* in the building of the church. ✳

THE PRAYER FOR STRENGTH

23 As soon as they were discharged they went back to their friends and told them everything that the chief priests and
24 elders had said. When they heard it, they raised their voices as one man and called upon God:

'Sovereign Lord, maker of heaven and earth and sea
25 and of everything in them, who by the Holy Spirit, through the mouth of David thy servant, didst say,

"Why did the Gentiles rage and the peoples lay their plots in vain?
26 The kings of the earth took their stand and the rulers made common cause

Against the Lord and against his Messiah."

27 They did indeed make common cause in this very city against thy holy servant Jesus whom thou didst anoint as Messiah. Herod and Pontius Pilate conspired with the
28 Gentiles and peoples of Israel to do all the things which, under thy hand and by thy decree, were foreordained.
29 And now, O Lord, mark their threats, and enable thy
30 servants to speak thy word with all boldness. Stretch out thy hand to heal and cause signs and wonders to be done through the name of thy holy servant Jesus.'

31 When they had ended their prayer, the building where they were assembled rocked, and all were filled with the Holy Spirit and spoke the word of God with boldness.

✻ Another dramatic picture. This time it is the nucleus of the persecuted church praying for courage to *enable thy servants to speak thy word with all boldness.*

24–5. The address to God recalls Hezekiah's prayer (Isa. 37: 16–20).

25–6. The messianic text from Ps. 2: 1–2 was an obvious choice for the early church. The original meaning of *Messiah* in the Psalm is clearly 'the king', but for the early church the whole Psalm spoke of the passion of Christ.

by the Holy Spirit is omitted by some authorities. The Greek in this clause is uncertain.

31. God's Holy Spirit is present with power. (Cf. Isa. 6: 4, 'the foundations of the thresholds were moved at the voice of him that cried'.) There is no need to regard this as an alternative to the story of the coming of the Spirit in 2: 1–4. It was now a time of renewal through prayer and the Spirit inspired them afresh. ✻

THE COMMON LIFE

The whole body of believers was united in heart and soul. 32 Not a man of them claimed any of his possessions as his own, but everything was held in common, while the 33 apostles bore witness with great power to the resurrection of the Lord Jesus. They were all held in high esteem; for 34 they had never a needy person among them, because all who had property in land or houses sold it, brought the proceeds of the sale, and laid the money at the feet of the 35 apostles; it was then distributed to any who stood in need.

For instance, Joseph, surnamed by the apostles Barnabas 36 (which means 'Son of Exhortation'), a Levite, by birth a Cypriot, owned an estate, which he sold; he brought the 37 money, and laid it at the apostles' feet.

But there was another man, called Ananias, with his **5**

2 wife Sapphira, who sold a property. With the full knowledge of his wife he kept back part of the purchase-money,
3 and part he brought and laid at the apostles' feet. But
Peter said, 'Ananias, how was it that Satan so possessed
your mind that you lied to the Holy Spirit, and kept back
4 part of the price of the land? While it remained, did it
not remain yours? When it was turned into money, was
it not still at your own disposal? What made you think
of doing this thing? You have lied not to men but to
5 God.' When Ananias heard these words he dropped
6 dead; and all the others who heard were awestruck. The
younger men rose and covered his body, then carried him
out and buried him.

7 About three hours passed, and then his wife came in,
8 unaware of what had happened. Peter turned to her and
said, 'Tell me, were you paid such and such a price for
9 the land?' 'Yes,' she said, 'that was the price.' Then
Peter said, 'Why did you both conspire to put the Spirit
of the Lord to the test? Hark! there at the door are the
footsteps of those who buried your husband; and they
10 will carry you away.' And suddenly she dropped dead
at his feet. When the young men came in, they found her
dead; and they carried her out and buried her beside her
11 husband. And a great awe fell upon the whole church,
12 and upon all who heard of these events; and many remarkable and wonderful things took place among the people
at the hands of the apostles.

* This is a brilliant picture of contrast. What could be more
idyllic than *the whole body of believers…united in heart and
soul*? There was no selfishness, no poverty. The church was
carrying out the words of Jesus recorded by Luke alone. 'Sell

your possessions and give in charity. Provide for yourselves purses that do not wear out, and never-failing wealth in heaven, where no thief can get near it, no moth destroy it' (Luke 12: 33). Cf. 2: 44. Barnabas is used as an example of a disciple at his best. *But* there was another man. Luke would have made a wonderful television producer. First, his camera is on Barnabas offering his goods at the apostles' feet. A moment later Ananias is a corpse before them. No wonder the viewers *were awestruck*. Once again Luke is busy with his introductions —first Barnabas and then Ananias and Sapphira.

36–7. Joseph is described carefully—a hellenistic Jew, of Levitical family from Cyprus—perhaps because later he accompanied Paul on his first trip which began through his home island. The interpretation of the name Barnabas as *Son of Exhortation* does not correspond to any known meaning for the name. It might mean 'Son of a Prophet'. Perhaps this unexpected interpretation proves that Luke did not know Aramaic. Whatever its origin the interpretation provides an apt character-study of Barnabas (cf. 9: 27). Col. 4: 10 refers to Mark as 'the cousin of Barnabas'.

5: 1–12. The contrast of this story with that of Barnabas is highly sensational. The sin was not the holding back of part of the purchase-money but the pretending to hand over the whole. Furthermore, the lie was to *the Holy Spirit* himself. The story might be compared with that of Achan (Josh. 7), who kept back part of the offering dedicated to God and was destroyed with his family and possessions. The deaths of these two must have been alarming, whatever the exact details. One gets the impression from Luke's account that Peter did not hesitate to make use of the alarm. *Many remarkable and wonderful things took place among the people at the hands of the apostles* (verse 12). ✻

A SECOND SKIRMISH

They used to meet by common consent in Solomon's
13 Cloister, no one from outside their number venturing to
join with them. But people in general spoke highly of
14 them, and more than that, numbers of men and women
15 were added to their ranks as believers in the Lord. In the
end the sick were actually carried out into the streets and
laid there on beds and stretchers, so that even the shadow
16 of Peter might fall on one or another as he passed by; and
the people from the towns round Jerusalem flocked in,
bringing those who were ill or harassed by unclean spirits,
and all of them were cured.

17 Then the High Priest and his colleagues, the Sadducean
party as it then was, were goaded into action by jealousy.
18 They proceeded to arrest the apostles, and put them in
19 official custody. But an angel of the Lord opened the
prison doors during the night, brought them out, and
20 said, 'Go, take your place in the temple and speak to the
people, and tell them about this new life and all it means.'
21 Accordingly they entered the temple at daybreak and
went on with their teaching.

When the High Priest arrived with his colleagues they
summoned the 'Sanhedrin', that is, the full senate of the
Israelite nation, and sent to the jail to fetch the prisoners.
22 But the police who went to the prison failed to find them
23 there, so they returned and reported, 'We found the jail
securely locked at every point, with the warders at their
posts by the doors, but when we opened them we found
24 no one inside.' When they heard this, the Controller of
the Temple and the chief priests were wondering what

could have become of them, and then a man arrived with 25
the report, 'Look! the men you put in prison are there
in the temple teaching the people.' At that the Controller 26
went off with the police and fetched them, but without
using force for fear of being stoned by the people.

So they brought them and stood them before the 27
Council; and the High Priest began his examination. 'We 28
expressly ordered you', he said, 'to desist from teaching
in that name; and what has happened? You have filled
Jerusalem with your teaching, and you are trying to make
us responsible for that man's death.' Peter replied for 29
himself and the apostles: 'We must obey God rather than
men. The God of our fathers raised up Jesus whom you 30
had done to death by hanging him on a gibbet. He it is 31
whom God has exalted with his own right hand as leader
and saviour, to grant Israel repentance and forgiveness of
sins. And we are witnesses to all this, and so is the Holy 32
Spirit given by God to those who are obedient to him.'

This touched them on the raw, and they wanted to put 33
them to death. But a member of the Council rose to his 34
feet, a Pharisee called Gamaliel, a teacher of the law held
in high regard by all the people. He moved that the men
be put outside for a while. Then he said, 'Men of Israel, 35
be cautious in deciding what to do with these men. Some 36
time ago Theudas came forward, claiming to be some-
body, and a number of men, about four hundred, joined
him. But he was killed and his whole following was
broken up and disappeared. After him came Judas the 37
Galilean at the time of the census; he induced some people
to revolt under his leadership, but he too perished and his
whole following was scattered. And so now: keep clear 38

of these men, I tell you; leave them alone. For if this idea
of theirs or its execution is of human origin, it will col-
39 lapse; but if it is from God, you will never be able to put
them down, and you risk finding yourselves at war with
God.'

40   They took his advice. They sent for the apostles and
had them flogged; then they ordered them to give up
41 speaking in the name of Jesus, and discharged them. So
the apostles went out from the Council rejoicing that they
had been found worthy to suffer indignity for the sake of
42 the Name. And every day they went steadily on with
their teaching in the temple and in private houses, telling
the good news of Jesus the Messiah.

✶ The success of the apostles, combined with their flagrant
disobedience to the rulers' commands (4: 18), *goaded* the
Sadducean party *into action by jealousy*.

12–14. *Solomon's Cloister* seems to have been the regular
meeting-place (cf. 3: 11). These three verses read strangely for,
although *no one from outside their number* ventured *to join with
them…numbers of men and women were added to their ranks as
believers in the Lord*. The N.E.B. footnote offers an alternative
translation…'Cloister. Although others did not venture to
join them, the common people spoke highly of them, and an
ever-increasing number of believers, both men and women,
were added to the Lord.'

15–16. The power of the Spirit is again apparent, working
through Peter as the leader. The account closely resembles
Mark's account of Jesus in Mark 6: 55–6.

18. The situation was becoming more dangerous so the
apostles were *put…in official custody* this time (cf. 4: 3).

19–21. Whatever was the apostles' means of escape, there
is no doubt that Luke regarded it as miraculous, as he did
Peter's release (12: 6–11) and that of Paul and Silas (16: 25–34).

21. The N.E.B. is right to explain the Sanhedrin as *the full senate of the Israelite nation.* One council is involved, not two. The officials are the same as those mentioned in the first skirmish (4: 1).

26. The support of the people for the apostles is clearly known to their rulers, and in the charge (verse 28) the High Priest is fearful of revenge for Jesus' death.

29–32. Peter's reply is as challenging as before (4: 10): *We must obey God rather than men. The God of our fathers raised up Jesus whom you had done to death!* God raised up this Jesus *with* (or at) *his own right hand* to be the *leader and saviour* of his people.

32. The apostles are eyewitnesses of this and the Holy Spirit confirms it.

33. This obviously infuriated the Sanhedrin. The N.E.B. *touched them on the raw* is a colourful translation for 'sawn in two' or 'cut to the heart'.

34–9. Then through the fury of the Council one of its members rose with quiet dignity. This is one of Luke's most gracious introductions. The Pharisee, Gamaliel, was highly honoured by all. A famous teacher himself and tutor of Paul (22: 3), he was a descendant of Hillel, the leader of the more open-minded school, as opposed to Shammai, the more conservative. He asks for the prisoners to be withdrawn and then in his wisdom he counsels caution. If the movement has not God behind it, it will sink into oblivion anyway; if it has, nothing can stop it.

36. According to Josephus (*Antiquities* xx. 5. 1) the rebellion of Theudas took place later, about A.D. 44–5 when Fadus was procurator of Judaea. Unless there was an earlier rebellion by someone also named Theudas, Luke would seem to be in error in assigning this reference to Gamaliel.

37. Judas the Galilean led a revolt in A.D. 6 when Quirinius was Roman legate of Syria. The census he carried out was ten years after the one Luke mentions in Luke 2: 2. It does not seem likely that Luke was confused by Josephus' reference

47

to the death of the *sons* of Judas of Galilee in the paragraph immediately following the one on Theudas, and thus any attempt to date the passage after the publication of Josephus' *Antiquities* in about A.D. 94 would be equally doubtful (see above, p. 13). If the revolt of Judas the Galilean is the one in A.D. 6 then his followers became the Zealot party and did not collapse.

38–9. Whatever events Gamaliel had in mind his point is quite clear: *if this idea of theirs or its execution is of human origin, it will collapse; but if it is from God, you will never be able to put them down, and you risk finding yourselves at war with God.*

40. The flogging was normal practice in such cases, as Paul says in 22: 19. Cf. Mark 13: 9, where Jesus warned them that this would happen.

41–2. It was a triumph for the apostles who went on proclaiming that Jesus was the Messiah. ✲

✲ ✲ ✲ ✲ ✲ ✲ ✲ ✲ ✲ ✲ ✲ ✲ ✲

The Church Moves Outwards

THE APPOINTMENT OF THE SEVEN

6 DURING THIS PERIOD, when disciples were growing in number, there was disagreement between those of them who spoke Greek and those who spoke the language of the Jews. The former party complained that their widows were being overlooked in the daily distribu-
2 tion. So the Twelve called the whole body of disciples together and said, 'It would be a grave mistake for us to
3 neglect the word of God in order to wait at table. Therefore, friends, look out seven men of good reputation from your number, men full of the Spirit and of wisdom, and we

will appoint them to deal with these matters, while we 4
devote ourselves to prayer and to the ministry of the
Word.' This proposal proved acceptable to the whole 5
body. They elected Stephen, a man full of faith and of
the Holy Spirit, Philip, Prochorus, Nicanor, Timon, Par-
menas, and Nicolas of Antioch, a former convert to
Judaism. These they presented to the apostles, who prayed 6
and laid their hands on them.

The word of God now spread more and more widely; 7
the number of disciples in Jerusalem went on increasing
rapidly, and very many of the priests adhered to the Faith.

* Here is seen a development in the organization of the infant
church. The Twelve needed assistants who would be particularly responsible for the charitable side of the work whilst they
themselves concentrated on prayer and preaching. The Seven
were appointed and the church continued to grow rapidly.

1. The church was still composed of Jews, but there had
arisen a division between the Greek-speaking section, or Hellenists, who were descendants of Jews who had lived abroad
and adopted Greek language and ideas but who were themselves now living again in Palestine, and the Hebrew section,
who had remained resident in Palestine all the time. It would
seem that a rota of *widows* had been established and that they
were in receipt of relief from the *daily distribution*. The *distribution* to any in need is described as part of the work of the
young church in 4: 35. It followed the normal practice of the
synagogue.

disciples, the normal word for Christians in the Gospels, is
soon replaced by 'brethren' or 'saints'.

2-4. The Seven were to be chosen by the whole assembly
and appointed by the Twelve. They were to be men of known
good character, filled with wisdom and the Holy Spirit, as
the Twelve were themselves at Pentecost. The Spirit would

show himself, not only in their personal reputation and ability to fulfil the immediate practical tasks, but also in signs and wonders and in preaching and teaching (Stephen, 6: 8, 10).

5. The names of all the Seven are Greek. They were probably all Hellenists and this no doubt indicates a desire to appease the Greek section. Acts refers only to the activity of Stephen and of Philip (6: 8 — 8: 40), but Philip is again mentioned as 'the evangelist' in 21: 8–9. Nicolas of Antioch was *a former convert to Judaism* or proselyte like those present at Pentecost (2: 10).

6. After they had been presented to the apostles by the disciples, the Seven received their commission by the laying on of the apostles' hands with prayer.

7. The church grew rapidly and the inclusion of *very many of the priests* was, from its particular mention, something of an achievement. It shows that even the temple priesthood was being attracted by *the Faith*. ✴

THE ARREST OF STEPHEN

8 Stephen, who was full of grace and power, began to work
9 great miracles and signs among the people. But some members of the synagogue called the Synagogue of Freedmen, comprising Cyrenians and Alexandrians and people from Cilicia and Asia, came forward and argued
10 with Stephen, but could not hold their own against the
11 inspired wisdom with which he spoke. They then put up men who alleged that they had heard him make blas-
12 phemous statements against Moses and against God. They stirred up the people and the elders and doctors of the law, set upon him and seized him, and brought him
13 before the Council. They produced false witnesses who said, 'This man is for ever saying things against this holy
14 place and against the Law. For we have heard him say

that Jesus of Nazareth will destroy this place and alter the customs handed down to us by Moses.' And all who were 15 sitting in the Council fixed their eyes on him, and his face appeared to them like the face of an angel.

✻ Stephen's place in the early church was clearly very important, for the author devotes much space to him. His influence went far beyond the distribution of charity. He worked *great miracles and signs among the people* (verse 8) and spoke with *inspired wisdom* (verse 10). Stephen's activity, his trial and his martyrdom led to the spread of the church among the Gentiles and paved the way for Paul.

9. The N.E.B. clearly suggests that there was only one synagogue of foreign Freedmen (*Libertini* = slaves who had acquired their freedom). The R.V. leaves the number confused. The members included Africans on the one hand and Asiatics on the other, some from Paul's own home district (Tarsus).

11. Alleging that he blasphemed against Moses and against God, false witnesses challenged Stephen, as they had Jesus (Matt. 26: 60–1).

12. The result of these accusations was a public riot. *The elders and doctors of the law* (Pharisees) took advantage of the situation and brought Stephen before the Sanhedrin.

13–14. The charge is the natural sequel to that brought against Jesus: that Stephen had said that Jesus of Nazareth would destroy the Temple and the Mosaic Law. It is not clear whether Stephen was the victim of mob violence or properly tried in a court of law.

15. Stephen's obvious inspiration transfixed the Council. The appearance of Stephen's face is reminiscent of that of the man of God who came to Manoah's wife (Judg. 13: 6, 'his countenance was like the countenance of the angel of God'), or that of Moses himself (Exod. 34: 29). Perhaps the Council had in mind Eccles. 8: 1, 'A man's wisdom maketh his face to shine'. ✻

' WHEN YOU ARE BROUGHT BEFORE SYNAGOGUES AND
STATE AUTHORITIES, DO NOT BEGIN WORRYING ABOUT
HOW YOU WILL CONDUCT YOUR DEFENCE OR WHAT YOU
WILL SAY. FOR WHEN THE TIME COMES THE HOLY SPIRIT
WILL INSTRUCT YOU WHAT TO SAY' (Luke 12: 11–12)

7 1,2 Then the High Priest asked, 'Is this so?' And he said,
'My brothers, fathers of this nation, listen to me. The
God of glory appeared to Abraham our ancestor while he
3 was in Mesopotamia, before he had settled in Harran, and
said: "Leave your country and your kinsfolk and come
4 away to a land that I will show you." Thereupon he left
the land of the Chaldaeans and settled in Harran. From
there, after his father's death, God led him to migrate to
5 this land where you now live. He gave him nothing in
it to call his own, not one yard; but promised to give it
in possession to him and his descendants after him, though
6 he was then childless. God spoke in these terms: "Abraham's descendants shall live as aliens in a foreign land,
7 held in slavery and oppression for four hundred years. And
I will pass judgement", said God, "on the nation whose
slaves they are; and after that they shall come out free,
8 and worship me in this place." He then gave him the
covenant of circumcision, and so, after Isaac was born,
he circumcised him on the eighth day; and Isaac begot
Jacob, and Jacob the twelve patriarchs.

9 'The patriarchs out of jealousy sold Joseph into slavery
10 in Egypt, but God was with him and rescued him from
all his troubles. He also gave him a presence and powers
of mind which so commended him to Pharaoh king of
Egypt, that he appointed him chief administrator for
Egypt and the whole of the royal household.

'But famine struck the whole of Egypt and Canaan, 11 and caused great hardship; and our ancestors could find nothing to eat. But Jacob heard that there was food in 12 Egypt and sent our fathers there. This was their first visit. On the second visit Joseph was recognized by his brothers, 13 and his family connexions were disclosed to Pharaoh. So 14 Joseph sent an invitation to his father Jacob and all his relatives, seventy-five persons altogether; and Jacob went 15 down into Egypt. There he ended his days, as also our 16 forefathers did. Their remains were later removed to Shechem and buried in the tomb which Abraham had bought and paid for from the clan of Emmor at Shechem.

'Now as the time approached for God to fulfil the 17 promise he had made to Abraham, our nation in Egypt grew and increased in numbers. At length another king, 18 who knew nothing of Joseph, ascended the throne of Egypt. He made a crafty attack on our race, and cruelly 19 forced our ancestors to expose their children so that they should not survive. At this time Moses was born. He 20 was a fine child, and pleasing to God. For three months he was nursed in his father's house, and when he was exposed, Pharaoh's daughter herself adopted him and 21 brought him up as her own son. So Moses was trained 22 in all the wisdom of the Egyptians, a powerful speaker and a man of action.

'He was approaching the age of forty, when it occurred 23 to him to look into the conditions of his fellow-country-men the Israelites. He saw one of them being ill-treated, 24 so he went to his aid, and avenged the victim by striking down the Egyptian. He thought his fellow-country- 25 men would understand that God was offering them

deliverance through him, but they did not understand.
26 The next day he came upon two of them fighting,
and tried to bring them to make up their quarrel. "My
men," he said, "you are brothers; why are you ill-treating
27 one another?" But the man who was at fault pushed him
away. "Who set you up as a ruler and judge over us?"
28 he said. "Are you going to kill me like the Egyptian you
29 killed yesterday?" At this Moses fled the country and settled
in Midianite territory. There two sons were born to him.

30   'After forty years had passed, an angel appeared to him
in the flame of a burning bush in the desert near Mount
31 Sinai. Moses was amazed at the sight. But as he approached to look closely, the voice of the Lord was heard:
32 "I am the God of your fathers, the God of Abraham,
Isaac, and Jacob." Moses was terrified and dared not look.
33 Then the Lord said to him, "Take off your shoes; the
34 place where you are standing is holy ground. I have
indeed seen how my people are oppressed in Egypt and
have heard their groans; and I have come down to rescue
them. Up, then; let me send you to Egypt."

35   'This Moses, whom they had rejected with the words,
"Who made you ruler and judge?"—this very man was
commissioned as ruler and liberator by God himself,
speaking through the angel who appeared to him in the
36 bush. It was Moses who led them out, working miracles
and signs in Egypt, at the Red Sea, and for forty years in
37 the desert. It was he again who said to the Israelites, "God
will raise up a prophet for you from among yourselves
38 as he raised me." He it was who, when they were
assembled there in the desert, conversed with the angel
who spoke to him on Mount Sinai, and with our fore-

fathers; he received the living utterances of God, to pass on to us.

'But our forefathers would not accept his leadership. 39 They thrust him aside. They wished themselves back in Egypt, and said to Aaron, "Make us gods to go before 40 us. As for that Moses, who brought us out of Egypt, we do not know what has become of him." That was when 41 they made the bull-calf, and offered sacrifice to the idol, and held a feast in honour of the thing their hands had made. But God turned away from them and gave them 42 over to the worship of the hosts of heaven, as it stands written in the book of the prophets: "Did you bring me victims and offerings those forty years in the desert, you house of Israel? No, you carried aloft the shrine of 43 Moloch and the star of the god Rephan, the images which you had made for your adoration. I will banish you beyond Babylon."

'Our forefathers had the Tent of the Testimony in the 44 desert, as God commanded when he told Moses to make it after the pattern which he had seen. Our fathers of the 45 next generation, with Joshua, brought it with them when they dispossessed the nations whom God drove out before them, and there it was until the time of David. David 46 found favour with God and asked to be allowed to provide a dwelling-place for the God of Jacob; but it was Solomon 47 who built him a house. However, the Most High does 48 not live in houses made by men: as the prophet says, "Heaven is my throne and earth my footstool. What kind 49 of house will you build for me, says the Lord; where is my resting-place? Are not all these things of my own 50 making?"

51 'How stubborn you are, heathen still at heart and deaf
to the truth! You always fight against the Holy Spirit.
52 Like fathers, like sons. Was there ever a prophet whom
your fathers did not persecute? They killed those who
foretold the coming of the Righteous One; and now you
53 have betrayed him and murdered him, you who received
the Law as God's angels gave it to you, and yet have not
kept it.'

✶ The Holy Spirit did not, as might have been expected,
instruct Stephen (or Luke through the mouth of Stephen) to
enter upon a defence against the charges brought against him,
but provided instead a summary of the work of the Spirit
through Israel's history to that hour. The speech is, therefore,
a missionary one. Like all martyrs who were given the opportunity, Stephen uses his to expound the faith for which he
stood condemned. The length of the speech is sufficient indication of the importance Luke attached to it. So far the work
of the apostles had been largely concerned with the Jews of
Palestine; now, with the appointment of the Seven, the church
was moving outwards—first to the Hellenists of the Diaspora
(or Dispersion, i.e. Jews from outside Palestine). Stephen now
found himself in conflict with them over the meaning of the
Temple and the Law. They were unable to see that Jesus of
Nazareth was the Messiah for whom the whole history of
Israel was a preparation. Yet their rejection of Jesus was in the
tradition of Israel. *The patriarchs out of jealousy sold Joseph into
slavery in Egypt, but God was with him and rescued him from all
his troubles* (verses 9–10). *This Moses, whom they had rejected with
the words, 'Who made you ruler and judge?'—this very man was
commissioned as ruler and liberator by God himself* (verse 35).
These were 'types' or symbolic forerunners of *the Righteous
One* whom *you have betrayed...and murdered* (verse 52).
Abraham, Joseph, Moses were all, like Jesus, called by God;
Joseph and Moses were, like him, both rejected. In one

way or another they symbolized or 'prefigured' the Messiah. Events in their lives were regarded as typical or representative of those in the life of Christ. In varying ways they foreshadowed him. But instead of seeing the outcome of the work of the Holy Spirit through Israel's history in Jesus, the Jews had become obsessed with the idea of the Temple as God's house, though *the Most High does not live in houses made by men* (verse 48), and with *the Law as God's angels gave it to you*, but you *have not kept it* (verse 53). There could hardly have been a more direct challenge to Israel's most cherished institutions. 'This touched them on the raw and they ground their teeth with fury' (verse 54). It was the end of phase one in the growth of the church in Acts. Luke had concluded his Gospel with the disciples spending 'all their time in the temple praising God' (24: 53). Stephen's speech marks the end of this period of co-existence. Henceforth it was 'a time of violent persecution for the church in Jerusalem' (8: 1).

2. *The God of glory*: Ps. 29: 3.

3. Abraham's call (see Gen. 12: 1) came at Haran but 15: 7 explains that it was God who brought him originally from Ur.

5. Abraham had no possession in Canaan—*not one yard*. He depended on God's promise.

6–7. Gen. 15: 13–14.

9–10. The comparison with the rulers' attitude to Jesus is clear. God rescued Jesus as he did Joseph.

16. There is some confusion regarding the burial-place. Josh. 24: 32 says Joseph was buried in Shechem in the tomb 'which Jacob bought of the sons of Hamor' (cf. Gen. 33: 19). Jacob was buried at Hebron in the field Abraham bought for a buryingplace (Gen. 50: 13; 23: 19). The reference to the burial-ground in Shechem, now in Samaritan territory, would further incense his hearers. Jacob also prefigured Christ in that he was buried in a tomb bought by someone else.

17–43. Moses is the second 'type' of Christ, and this section of the speech emphasizes his rejection. *Our forefathers would not accept his leadership. They thrust him aside* (verse 39).

22, 25. These additional touches to the account in Exodus are to be found in Josephus, *Antiquities* II. 9.7 and Philo, *De Vita Moysis*. In Jewish circles of this period there was much edifying expansion of the old stories—some of this is to be found in contemporary works like *Jubilees*, some in the Targums (Aramaic paraphrases of the Hebrew scriptures), some in Jewish authors like Josephus and Philo, some in the New Testament—all drawing on a rich common tradition.

29. In Exod. 2: 15 Moses' flight is owing to fear of Pharaoh.

30–4. The call of Moses at the bush in Exod. 3 is the prototype or symbolic foreshadowing of God's words to Jesus at his baptism (Luke 3: 21–2). *This very man was commissioned as ruler and liberator by God himself* (verse 35).

37. See 3: 22, and Deut. 18: 15. The importance of this text is obvious in view of the argument.

38. The N.E.B. uses the verb *assembled* to translate the noun *ecclesia*, 'church' (R.V.) or 'congregation' (R.V. margin; R.S.V.). Perhaps 'assembly' is the word, as in Deut. 18: 16, where Moses was mediator between God and his people.

39. *But our forefathers would not accept his leadership*: the comparison with Jesus is pressed home again.

40–2a. Israel rebels against God and turns to the worship of idols. *As for that Moses...we do not know what has become of him* (see Exod. 32: 1, 23). God's appeals to Israel had been refused so he let them go their own way.

42b–3. Amos 5: 25–7. The quotation is used to refer to Israel's idolatry in the wilderness whereas the prophet had been concerned with later developments, particularly worship of stars. *The shrine of Moloch* seems to be a mistranslation for 'Siccuth your king' (an Assyrian god). *Rephan* is substituted for 'Chiun' (the Assyrian name for Saturn). The substitution of *Babylon* for Damascus brought the punishment nearer home in time, and perhaps infuriated the court by a veiled reference to their own subordinate position to their present overlord.

In later times 'Babylon' was used to mean Rome; but probably does not have that meaning here (cf. I Pet. 5: 13; Rev. 18: 2). In these verses the quotation follows the LXX and this differs from the Hebrew. The exact meaning and interpretation of this passage of Amos is highly uncertain, though it clearly indicates idolatrous practices whether in the wilderness or later.

44–50. The presence of God in the midst of Israel was exemplified by *the Tent of the Testimony* moving about with them, until after Joshua had brought it into the promised land, David had *asked to be allowed to provide* a more permanent *dwelling-place for the God of Jacob*, and Solomon had built it. But now their reliance on the Temple was almost a new idolatry.

44. *Tent of the Testimony*: the N.E.B. translation for 'tent of witness' (R.S.V.) or Tabernacle (see Exod. 36).

46. Some manuscripts read 'house of Jacob' but *God of Jacob* would seem more correct.

49–50. The quotation is from Isa. 66: 1–2.

51–3. Stephen's work was almost done. His hearers could see where it was leading. As their forefathers had rejected the working of the Holy Spirit in the past, so they had in the present. *You always fight against the Holy Spirit*. You, who have had all the advantages of a God-given Law, have refused to see that it, like the Temple, has been superseded by Christ. You killed the prophets who foretold him and *now you have betrayed him and murdered him*.

52. *Righteous One*: see 3: 14. ✳

PERSECUTION HAS BEGUN

This touched them on the raw and they ground their 54 teeth with fury. But Stephen, filled with the Holy Spirit, 55 and gazing intently up to heaven, saw the glory of God, and Jesus standing at God's right hand. 'Look,' he said, 56

'there is a rift in the sky; I can see the Son of Man standing
57 at God's right hand!' At this they gave a great shout and
58 stopped their ears. Then they made one rush at him and,
flinging him out of the city, set about stoning him. The
witnesses laid their coats at the feet of a young man named
59 Saul. So they stoned Stephen, and as they did so, he called
60 out, 'Lord Jesus, receive my spirit.' Then he fell on his
knees and cried aloud, 'Lord, do not hold this sin against
8 them', and with that he died. And Saul was among those
who approved of his murder.

* The anger of the Sanhedrin was to be expected, and it was
made worse by Stephen's claim, which they thought blasphemy, that he could see Jesus exalted *at God's right hand*
(verse 56). The execution is hardly a decision of the court.
It is rather mob violence. On Stephen's side, the Holy Spirit
is there all the time (verse 55). For Luke the most perfect
martyrdom was that of Jesus (Luke 23: 26–48); now his
servant follows in Jesus' footsteps, committing to him his
spirit (verse 59), as Jesus had committed his to the Father
(Luke 23: 46).

54. *touched them on the raw*: cf. 5: 33.

56. The vision granted to Stephen is very vivid. There is
a resemblance to the dramatic, prophetic visions of the heavenly
court seen by Micaiah (1 Kings 22: 19) and by Isaiah (Isa. 6).
Son of Man is found only here outside the Gospels. He is
standing, perhaps to receive his servant who has so fully
entered into his death. In Luke 22: 69 'the Son of Man' is
'seated at the right hand of Almighty God' in a position of
authority.

58. The stoning took place outside the city in accordance
with Num. 15: 35, and the witnesses cast the first stones (Deut.
17: 7).

60. Stephen's final prayer is the same as his master's (Luke
23: 34), and thus this verse supports the genuineness of the

gospel passage which is omitted in some manuscripts. The disciple imitated his master to the end.

58 and 8: 1. The suddenness of Saul's appearance on the stage of history is typical of Luke's introduction of his characters and reminiscent of the similar unannounced arrival of Elijah in 1 Kings 17: 1. For Luke the Holy Spirit is about to take a decisive part in Saul's life. As Stephen dies Saul is there; what Stephen has declared, Paul will eventually bring to its full deployment. ✳

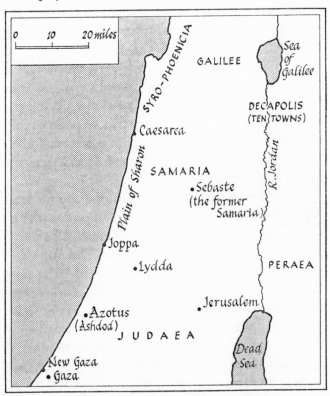

Philip in Samaria and the south, and Peter's visit to Cornelius at Caesarea

'AND SAMARIA' (1: 8)

This was the beginning of a time of violent persecution for the church in Jerusalem; and all except the apostles were scattered over the country districts of Judaea and
2 Samaria. Stephen was given burial by certain devout men,
3 who made a great lamentation for him. Saul, meanwhile, was harrying the church; he entered house after house, seizing men and women, and sending them to prison.

4 As for those who had been scattered, they went through
5 the country preaching the Word. Philip came down to a city in Samaria and began proclaiming the Messiah to
6 them. The crowds, to a man, listened eagerly to what Philip said, when they heard him and saw the miracles
7 that he performed. For in many cases of possession the unclean spirits came out with a great outcry; and many
8 paralysed and crippled folk were cured; and there was great joy in that city.

9 A man named Simon had been in the city for some time, and had swept the Samaritans off their feet with his
10 magical arts, claiming to be someone great. All of them, high and low, listened eagerly to him. 'This man', they said, 'is that power of God which is called "The Great
11 Power".' They listened because they had for so long been
12 carried away by his magic. But when they came to believe Philip with his good news about the kingdom of God and the name of Jesus Christ, they were baptized,
13 men and women alike. Even Simon himself believed, and was baptized, and thereupon was constantly in Philip's company. He was carried away when he saw the powerful signs and miracles that were taking place.

The apostles in Jerusalem now heard that Samaria had 14 accepted the word of God. They sent off Peter and John, who went down there and prayed for the converts, asking 15 that they might receive the Holy Spirit. For until then 16 the Spirit had not come upon any of them. They had been baptized into the name of the Lord Jesus, that and nothing more. So Peter and John laid their hands on them and 17 they received the Holy Spirit.

When Simon saw that the Spirit was bestowed through 18 the laying on of the apostles' hands, he offered them money and said, 'Give me the same power too, so that 19 when I lay my hands on anyone, he will receive the Holy Spirit.' 'You and your money,' said Peter sternly, 'may 20 you come to a bad end, for thinking God's gift is for sale! You have no part nor lot in this, for you are dishonest 21 with God. Repent of this wickedness and pray the Lord 22 to forgive you for imagining such a thing. I can see that 23 you are doomed to taste the bitter fruit and wear the fetters of sin.' Simon answered, 'Pray to the Lord for me 24 yourselves and ask that none of the things you have spoken of may fall upon me.'

And so, after giving their testimony and speaking the 25 word of the Lord, they took the road back to Jerusalem, bringing the good news to many Samaritan villages on the way.

✻ Before the conversion of Saul, the Holy Spirit had another task on hand in fulfilment of Jesus' command (1: 8): Samaria—a new field of action for the growing church foreshadowed by Jesus' own visits there (see Luke 9: 52–62; 17: 11–19; John 4: 1–42). The work of the Spirit never ceases. Every opportunity is used. *Violent persecution for the church in*

Jerusalem meant that *all except the apostles were scattered over the country districts of Judaea and Samaria*; but not in hiding for fear: *as for those who had been scattered, they went through the country preaching the Word.*

2. Stephen's *burial by certain devout men* is a further correspondence with the death of Jesus and his burial by Joseph of Arimathaea and Nicodemus (Luke 23: 50–3; John 19: 38–42). The *great lamentation* at Stephen's burial may seem a little strange in view of Saul's systematic attack (verse 3) but no precise chronology is implied.

5–8. *Philip*, the second of the Seven in the list in 6: 5. His mission to Samaria was a highly important move. The Samaritans were regarded by the Jews as a mixed race with heretical beliefs, associated with the colonization of Samaria by the Assyrians in 722 B.C. But the real break came much later: each community claimed the Law (the first five books of the Bible) and regarded its own sacred place—Jerusalam or Gerizim, near Samaria—as the true one. Political antagonism made the situation even worse (see *Understanding the New Testament*, in this series, pp. 13, 21, 38). Philip's teaching was accompanied by signs like Stephen's (6: 8).

8. The 'unaffected joy' (2: 46) of the first days in Jerusalem was now felt in this Samaritan city.

9–13. Another new name. This time it was *Simon*, a sorcerer, and he represents the first occasion in Acts when the Way comes into contact with sorcery (cf. Elymas the sorcerer, 13: 8). How far this Simon is the one referred to by Justin (Christian martyr and apologist, *c.* 100–65, himself a native of Samaria) as one of the earliest gnostic leaders is very uncertain. Gnostic teaching developed in the second century and its adherents claimed a direct revelation of knowledge (*gnosis*) from God. Simon amazed his audience by his magical powers, *claiming to be someone great*.

10. '*The Great Power*': the Greek simply reads 'great'. *The Great Power* indicates that Simon was considered a manifestation of God by those who had heard him for so long.

13. Simon was amazed by Philip's acts and joined his company by being baptized. The double use of the verb *carried away* in verses 11 and 13 shows that Simon's reaction to Philip's *signs and miracles* was the same as that of the Samaritans to his own magic. He regarded Philip's work as merely a higher form of his own art. How little he understood of what was happening is clear from verses 18–24.

14–17. The Jerusalem church now sent the two apostles, Peter and John, who had taken so active a part in the extension of the church after Pentecost, to check what Philip had been doing. It seems that the Samaritans *had been baptized into the name of the Lord Jesus, that and nothing more.* They had been accepted as members but there had been no manifestation of the Spirit by the gift of tongues. Philip's introduction of the Way into Samaria was of tremendous importance to the church; its leaders had to make sure that it had the approval of the Holy Spirit. The result of laying on their hands (cf. 6: 6) proved to the apostles that it had.

18–25. Simon's amazement at what happened induced him to offer money to the apostles for the power to confer the Spirit.

20. Peter's denunciation of Simon reveals his own horror at the idea that *God's gift is for sale!* The curse seems almost irrevocable. Nonetheless Simon's sin is not beyond repentance (verse 22).

23. The N.E.B. footnote gives the literal translation—'you are for gall of bitterness and a fetter of unrighteousness.' The phrases are used in Deut. 29: 18 and Isa. 58: 6.

24. It is difficult to know whether Simon's reply indicates true repentance or terror. His action has been perpetuated in the word 'simony', meaning the purchase or sale of spiritual things.

25. The apostles returned to Jerusalem and themselves brought *the good news to many Samaritan villages on the way.* ✲

PHILIP IN THE SOUTH

26 Then the angel of the Lord said to Philip, 'Start out and go south to the road that leads down from Jerusalem to
27 Gaza.' (This is the desert road.) So he set out and was on his way when he caught sight of an Ethiopian. This man was a eunuch, a high official of the Kandake, or Queen, of Ethiopia, in charge of all her treasure. He had been to
28 Jerusalem on a pilgrimage and was now on his way home, sitting in his carriage and reading aloud the prophet
29 Isaiah. The Spirit said to Philip, 'Go and join the carriage'.
30 When Philip ran up he heard him reading the prophet Isaiah and said, 'Do you understand what you are
31 reading?' He said, 'How can I understand unless someone will give me the clue?' So he asked Philip to get in and sit beside him.

32 The passage he was reading was this: 'He was led like a sheep to be slaughtered; and like a lamb that is dumb
33 before the shearer, he does not open his mouth. He has been humiliated and has no redress. Who will be able to speak of his posterity? For his life is cut off and he is gone from the earth.'

34 'Now', said the eunuch to Philip, 'tell me, please, who it is that the prophet is speaking about here: himself or
35 someone else?' Then Philip began. Starting from this
36 passage, he told him the good news of Jesus. As they were going along the road, they came to some water. 'Look,' said the eunuch, 'here is water: what is there to prevent
38 my being baptized?'; and he ordered the carriage to stop. Then they both went down into the water, Philip and the
39 eunuch; and he baptized him. When they came up out

of the water the Spirit snatched Philip away, and the
eunuch saw no more of him, but went on his way well
content. Philip appeared at Azotus, and toured the coun- 40
try, preaching in all the towns till he reached Caesarea.

* Luke has to be selective in his examples of Philip's work;
first he chooses the Samaritans and now an Ethiopian. The
fact that this man *had been to Jerusalem on a pilgrimage* (verse 27)
indicates that he was a 'God-fearer', i.e. a Gentile interested
in Judaism but who had not become a proselyte. In the case
of the eunuch this latter step might not have been possible as
no castrated person could 'enter into the assembly of the Lord'
(Deut. 23: 1). The divine message (verse 26) causes Philip to
join the Ethiopian; starting from the passage in Isa. 53: 7–8,
which the man was reading, Philip *told him the good news of
Jesus* (verse 35). Thereupon the eunuch asks for baptism. After
it is over the Holy Spirit whisks Philip away to a new task
along the coast.

26. *Gaza*: the last town before the desert road to Egypt.
Old Gaza, one of the five ancient Philistine cities, two miles
from the sea, had been destroyed in 96 B.C. but a new Gaza
on the coast had been built under the Romans. The N.E.B.
assumes, probably rightly, that *desert* refers to the road rather
than the town.

27. *Ethiopia*: the kingdom of Meroe in southern Egypt,
the modern Sudan.

Kandake: a title, not a name; probably the dynastic title of
the queens of 'Ethiopia' who were in fact the rulers, whilst
their sons reigned nominally.

32–3. Isa. 53: 7–8 (LXX). This is part of the last of the
poems in Isaiah known as the 'Servant Songs'. Already they
were being used by Christians as prophecies of the Messiah.
This is Philip's answer to the eunuch's question. Christians
searched the scriptures to find confirmation of what they had
seen to be true (cf. Peter's speech after Pentecost, 2: 14–36;

and the Jews at Beroea who 'received the message with great eagerness, studying the scriptures every day to see whether it was as they said', 17: 11).

(37) The N.E.B. footnote gives this verse from later manuscripts: 'Philip said "If you whole-heartedly believe, it is permitted." He replied, "I believe that Jesus Christ is the Son of God."' This is probably an early baptismal confession.

39. *well content*: the R.V. and R.S.V. translation 'rejoicing' continues the idea of joy in the Spirit (verse 8) more clearly. There is no gift of the Spirit actually expressed here, though late texts seem conscious of the omission and add 'the Holy Spirit fell on the eunuch but the angel of the Lord' *snatched Philip away*.

40. *Azotus*: Ashdod—another of the five ancient Philistine cities, like Gaza, from where Philip continued his activities northwards until he reached Caesarea, where we find him in the only other reference to him in Acts (21: 8). *

SAUL

9 Meanwhile Saul was still breathing murderous threats against the disciples of the Lord. He went to the High
2 Priest and applied for letters to the synagogues at Damascus authorizing him to arrest anyone he found, men or women, who followed the new way, and bring them
3 to Jerusalem. While he was still on the road and nearing Damascus, suddenly a light flashed from the sky all
4 around him. He fell to the ground and heard a voice
5 saying, 'Saul, Saul, why do you persecute me?' 'Tell me, Lord,' he said, 'who you are.' The voice answered,
6 'I am Jesus, whom you are persecuting. But get up and go into the city, and you will be told what you have to
7 do.' Meanwhile the men who were travelling with him stood speechless; they heard the voice but could see no

one. Saul got up from the ground, but when he opened 8
his eyes he could not see; so they led him by the hand and
brought him into Damascus. He was blind for three days, 9
and took no food or drink.

There was a disciple in Damascus named Ananias. He 10
had a vision in which he heard the voice of the Lord:
'Ananias!' 'Here I am, Lord', he answered. The Lord 11
said to him, 'Go at once to Straight Street, to the house
of Judas, and ask for a man from Tarsus named Saul. You
will find him at prayer; he has had a vision of a man 12
named Ananias coming in and laying his hands on him
to restore his sight.' Ananias answered, 'Lord, I have 13
often heard about this man and all the harm he has done
to thy people in Jerusalem. And here he is with authority 14
from the chief priests to arrest all who invoke thy name.'
But the Lord said to him, 'You must go, for this man is 15
my chosen instrument to bring my name before the
nations and their kings, and before the people of Israel.
I myself will show him all that he must go through for 16
my name's sake.'

So Ananias went. He entered the house, laid his hands 17
on him and said, 'Saul, my brother, the Lord Jesus, who
appeared to you on your way here, has sent me to you
so that you may recover your sight, and be filled with the
Holy Spirit.' And immediately it seemed that scales fell 18
from his eyes, and he regained his sight. Thereupon he
was baptized, and afterwards he took food and his strength 19
returned.

He stayed some time with the disciples in Damascus.
Soon he was proclaiming Jesus publicly in the synagogues: 20
'This', he said, 'is the Son of God.' All who heard were 21

astounded. 'Is not this the man', they said, 'who was in Jerusalem trying to destroy those who invoke this name? Did he not come here for the sole purpose of arresting 22 them and taking them to the chief priests?' But Saul grew more and more forceful, and silenced the Jews of Damascus with his cogent proofs that Jesus was the Messiah.

23 As the days mounted up, the Jews hatched a plot against 24 his life; but their plans became known to Saul. They kept watch on the city gates day and night so that they might 25 murder him; but his converts took him one night and let him down by the wall, lowering him in a basket.

26 When he reached Jerusalem he tried to join the body of disciples there; but they were all afraid of him, because 27 they did not believe that he was really a convert. Barnabas, however, took him by the hand and introduced him to the apostles. He described to them how Saul had seen the Lord on his journey, and heard his voice, and how he had spoken out boldly in the name of Jesus at 28 Damascus. Saul now stayed with them, moving about 29 freely in Jerusalem. He spoke out boldly and openly in the name of the Lord, talking and debating with the Greek-speaking Jews. But they planned to murder him, 30 and when the brethren learned of this they escorted him to Caesarea and saw him off to Tarsus.

✽ Another dramatic scene. Luke has just given us an example of the work of one of the Seven and how all that Philip did to extend *the new way* (9: 2) was approved by the Holy Spirit. Now he rapidly changes the setting. In the centre of the stage is Saul *still breathing murderous threats against the disciples of the Lord*. The stories of Peter and Paul dovetail into each other at this point. The two great characters are kept surprisingly apart as the narrative proceeds (see above, pp. 1–2) but both, under the direction of the Holy Spirit, are learning what he has planned for them. They were to understand that 'God has granted life-giving repentance to the Gentiles also' (11: 18). Already the movement of the church away from a purely Jewish Christianity had been indicated by Philip's baptism of the Ethiopian eunuch, but something much more catastrophic would have to happen before the capture of God's *chosen instrument to bring my name before the nations and their kings* (verse 15). The importance attached by Luke to the conversion of Saul is apparent from the fact that it is recounted in detail three times in Acts—here; in Paul's speech from the steps leading to the barracks (22: 1–21); and in his defence before King Agrippa (26: 1–23). If we bear in mind the restrictions imposed upon an early writer by the possible length of a scroll and the cost of writing material, this repetition is of great significance. The genuineness of each account is equally clear from the slight variations in detail, whereas the outline of the story remains the same. Luke is not merely copying. He is using the 'call' as a re-authentication of Paul's status at important points in the story (cf. the similar repetition in the call of Amos 1: 1–2 and 7: 14–15). In his letters Paul himself is equally anxious to emphasize his divine commission (Gal. 1: 1, 12; 1 Cor. 11: 23; 15: 3). Luke is impressed by the work of the Holy Spirit in arresting Saul, whom he knew as his companion later on, and he intends the reader to be impressed as well.

The spread of *the new way* to Damascus shows how far the Christian church had progressed, spread perhaps by those who had witnessed the outpouring of the Spirit at Pentecost. To the Christians, still worshipping in the synagogues, came the official envoy from the Sanhedrin (verse 2).

1. *the Lord* takes up the description of Jesus as 'Lord and Messiah' in 2: 36.

2. *the new way* used by Christians in reference to themselves

(cf. 24: 14), linking them with Jesus, 'the way' (John 14: 6). The N.E.B. inserts *new* to distinguish from the O.T.: 'This is the way, walk ye in it' (Isa. 30: 21). In the O.T. the word 'way' almost equals religion in contexts such as this (cf. Jer. 10: 2; Isa. 35: 8).

3-9. The vision was so real to Saul that later he classed it as a resurrection appearance of Jesus. 'In the end he appeared even to me; though this birth of mine was monstrous, for I had persecuted the church' (1 Cor. 15: 8-9). Perhaps the result was not quite so sudden as it would appear. Saul had witnessed the work of Stephen (8: 1) and his energetic pursuit of the Christians may indicate a disturbed conscience. Now the Spirit struck. The light flashing *from the sky all around* is reminiscent of 'tongues like flames of fire' at Pentecost (2: 3). Saul's companions *heard the voice but could see no one*. In 22: 9 they 'saw the light, but did not hear the voice that spoke to me'. Obviously they were completely confused by what had happened. Saul's capture is complete. He acknowledges Jesus as *Lord* (verse 5), is stunned by his blindness and remains fasting (verses 8-9).

10-19. The place of Ananias in the story as the Spirit's agent is striking. This man, 'a devout observer of the Law and well spoken of by all the Jews of that place' (22: 12), though naturally concerned about the command he received, went at once to the house of Judas in Straight Street. The order was imperative. *You must go, for this man is my chosen instrument to bring my name before the nations and their kings, and before the people of Israel* (verse 15). He addressed Saul as *brother* (i.e. Christian), *laid his hands on him* as a token of membership of the Christian body, and Saul recovered his sight as a sign that the Holy Spirit had been given. The action of Ananias was confirmed by Saul's baptism and the end of his fast.

Luke's interest in people has been noted earlier (see pp. 1-2). Was Judas' house in Straight Street used for the breaking of bread (cf. 2: 46) and was Ananias a leader of the church there like Philemon at Colossae later on (Philem. 1–2)? The fascination of the way in which Luke introduces his characters is more from what he does *not* say than from what he does. Ananias' hesitation in going to Saul at Judas' house in Damascus contrasts interestingly with Barnabas' ready introduction of him to the disciples in Jerusalem (verse 27).

11. *Straight Street*: the name of the street is taken from its plan. It was very long and very straight.

You will find him at prayer: Luke's emphasis on prayer before a great event (cf. 1: 14; 1: 24).

Tarsus: an important city in Cilicia (see map, p. 89).

13. *thy people*: literally, 'saints' and so used by Paul (e.g. Rom. 15: 25–6) for Christians. The Greek word means 'devoted or consecrated to God'.

15. *my chosen instrument*: literally, 'vessel of election', i.e. God's, to carry his word to the Gentiles and witness before kings (e.g. Agrippa: chapter 26).

18. *scales*: not really evidence of Luke's medical knowledge. The word is used technically for skin diseases. Here it is more like shutters being removed from windows so that light is restored.

20–5. There is some discrepancy between the account of Saul's stay in Damascus here and in Galatians 1: 13–20, where he says that after his conversion 'without consulting any human being, without going up to Jerusalem to see those who were apostles before me, I went off at once to Arabia, and afterwards returned to Damascus' (verses 16–17). Presumably Luke did not know of an Arabian visit or regarded it as of personal importance to Saul alone, perhaps for meditation after his baptism (cf. Jesus in the wilderness, Luke 4: 1–13). Arabia was the kingdom of the Nabataeans south-east and east of Palestine. Its centre was at Petra (see map, p. 17).

20. According to his later custom Saul began his preaching in *the synagogues* (e.g. Pisidian Antioch, 13: 15 ff.). The content of his message was that Jesus was *the Son of God*, the promised Messiah. *Son of God* is used only in this place in Acts, but it

became a regular phrase in Paul's teaching (e.g. Gal. 2: 20, 'my present bodily life is lived by faith in the Son of God'; Rom. 1: 4, 'he was declared Son of God by a mighty act in that he rose from the dead').

21. *to destroy*: the R.V. and R.S.V. 'made havoc'. The Greek word is more dramatic than *to destroy*, e.g. ravage, lay waste.

23-4. The Jews were naturally alarmed at this extraordinary change of front and plotted to silence him. *Their plans became known to Saul*, as did 'the ambush' in 23: 16, i.e. the accomplishment of Paul's task necessitated the frustration of such plots.

24. Here it is the Jews who were watching *the city gates day and night so that they might murder him*. In 2 Cor. 11: 32 it was 'the commissioner of King Aretas' who 'kept the city under observation so as to have me arrested'. This was the ethnarch or leader of the Jewish community in Damascus, responsible to Aretas IV (9 B.C.–A.D. 40), the father-in-law of Herod Antipas and king of the Nabataeans (Arabia), who had at this time the overlordship of Damascus. As representative of the Jews the commissioner would be very willing to arrest Saul. Coins of Tiberius prove that Damascus was under direct Roman rule as late as A.D. 33-4. There is no evidence of strife between Rome and Aretas so it is likely he obtained control of Damascus by grant, probably from Caligula who succeeded Tiberius in A.D. 37. This suggests that Saul's escape took place about A.D. 38.

25. The escape in a basket is common to both accounts (see 2 Cor. 11: 33), though the word for basket differs. The N.E.B. is right to translate *his converts* instead of the R.V. and R.S.V. 'his disciples' which gives too much the impression that already a group of supporters had arisen.

26-30. According to Gal. 1: 18 it was 'three years' before Saul went up to Jerusalem where he stayed with Peter 'for a fortnight, without seeing any other of the apostles, except James the Lord's brother' (Gal. 1: 18-19). In Acts the visit to Jerusalem is after *the days mounted up* (verse 23) and, because

*the body of disciples...were all afraid of him, because they did not
believe that he was really a convert,* Barnabas, himself a hellenistic Jew (4: 36–7), *took him by the hand and introduced him to
the apostles.* This is a more public meeting than Galatians would
imply, for not only did Saul move *about freely in Jerusalem*
but he debated *with the Greek-speaking Jews* (Hellenists).
Stephen's work in this respect led to his martyrdom; so, when
plots were made against Saul (verse 29) the brethren got him
away to Caesarea and sent him home to Tarsus. This conforms
with Gal. 1: 21–2 where he is in 'the regions of Syria and
Cilicia' and had had no opportunity of seeing the Christians
of Judaea owing to his rapid departure from Jerusalem. In
comparing the accounts of Paul's conversion in Acts and
Galatians it must be remembered that neither is intended to
be a merely factual narrative; both represent interpretations
and traditions. Galatians is controversial and concerned with
the relationships between Jews and Gentiles in the church
and thus Paul is determined to assert his own independence
of all authority save Christ's. This leads to one presentation of
his conversion. Luke in Acts is concerned with the overall
development of the church and Paul's conversion is part of the
plan to include Gentiles in it. Hence a different interpretation
is placed on the same event. ✳

BACK TO PETER AND THE CHURCH IN PALESTINE:
'TO THE GENTILES ALSO' (11: 18)

✳ The great step was soon to be taken by Paul for his work
among Gentiles. It was therefore essential that the very
Jewish parent-church in Jerusalem should have a clear indication of what its attitude ought to be when it was asked to
approve this. Luke halts his account of Saul by leaving him
at work in his home district of Tarsus, and describes the way
in which Peter first, and then the rest of the apostles, were
brought to realize 'that God has granted life-giving repentance
to the Gentiles also' (11: 18). The story opens with the church

at peace in Judaea, Galilee and Samaria. The earlier persecution has died down and the Holy Spirit is quietly building up the strength of the church for the next move forward. 'Peter was making a general tour' (9: 32), perhaps confirming the work of other disciples as he and John had done earlier (8: 14–15). His vision at Joppa (10: 9–15) is all-important for the Gentile mission, as was his subsequent visit to Caesarea (10: 24–48), and his report to Jerusalem (11: 1–18). Throughout the section there is again the conscious feeling that the Spirit is powerfully at work. ✳

PETER'S GENERAL TOUR THROUGH LYDDA TO JOPPA

31 Meanwhile the church, throughout Judaea, Galilee, and Samaria, was left in peace to build up its strength. In the fear of the Lord, upheld by the Holy Spirit, it held on its way and grew in numbers.

32 Peter was making a general tour, in the course of which 33 he went down to visit God's people at Lydda. There he found a man named Aeneas who had been bed-ridden 34 with paralysis for eight years. Peter said to him, 'Aeneas, Jesus Christ cures you; get up and make your bed', and 35 immediately he stood up. All who lived in Lydda and Sharon saw him; and they turned to the Lord.

36 In Joppa there was a disciple named Tabitha (in Greek, Dorcas, meaning a gazelle), who filled her days with acts 37 of kindness and charity. At that time she fell ill and died; and they washed her body and laid it in a room upstairs. 38 As Lydda was near Joppa, the disciples, who had heard that Peter was there, sent two men to him with the urgent 39 request, 'Please come over to us without delay.' Peter thereupon went off with them. When he arrived they

took him upstairs to the room, where all the widows came and stood round him in tears, showing him the shirts and coats that Dorcas used to make while she was with them. Peter sent them all outside, and knelt down 40 and prayed. Then, turning towards the body, he said, 'Tabitha, arise.' She opened her eyes, saw Peter, and sat up. He gave her his hand and helped her to her feet. 41 Then he called the members of the congregation and the widows and showed her to them alive. The news spread 42 all over Joppa, and many came to believe in the Lord. Peter stayed on in Joppa for some time with one Simon, a 43 tanner.

* 31. *upheld by the Holy Spirit*. Literally, 'in the comfort of the Holy Spirit'. The Greek word is *paraclesis*, from which the title of the Spirit as paraclete, 'advocate' or 'one to plead our cause', is derived (John 14: 16; 1 John 2: 1).

Galilee: the only reference in Acts to Christians in Galilee.

32–5. The healing at Lydda of the paralytic Aeneas resembles the healing of the paralytic by Jesus in Luke 5: 18–26. Nothing is said of Aeneas' faith, but the fact that *immediately he stood up* when Peter told him *Jesus Christ cures you; get up and make your bed*, indicates his belief that Jesus, working through the Spirit, can cure him. The same Spirit that worked through Jesus in the Gospel works through his servant here.

32. *Lydda*: to the north-west of Jerusalem on the way to Joppa.

35. *Sharon*: the coastal plain from Joppa to Caesarea.

36–43. Peter moves on to Joppa, the port of Jerusalem, 39 miles by road to the north-west, at the request of the disciples (Christians), because one of their number, Tabitha, had died. The story of the raising closely resembles that of Jairus' daughter (Mark 5: 35–43). Not only are Jesus' actions similar to Peter's, but the Aramaic *Talitha cum* (Mark 5: 41), 'maiden arise', resembles *Tabitha, arise* here. Perhaps, too, the raising of the widow's son at Zarephath by Elijah (1 Kings 17: 17-24) and of the Shunammite's son by Elisha (2 Kings 4: 18-37) have affected the story. In all three accounts prayer forms an important part of the story and there is a close personal relationship between the living and the dead by word and action.

36. The N.E.B. explains the meaning of *Tabitha* (Aramaic) or *Dorcas* (Greek) as *gazelle*.

39. *widows.* Tabitha continued the charitable work amongst widows that is mentioned before the appointment of the Seven (6: 1). This does not imply an 'order' of widows as in 1 Tim. 5: 3-10.

42. *many came to believe in the Lord*: presumably from among the Jews in the district, but perhaps including others as well.

43. *Simon, a tanner*: to distinguish him from Simon Peter. ✻

CORNELIUS

10 At Caesarea there was a man named Cornelius, a centurion
2 in the Italian Cohort, as it was called. He was a religious man, and he and his whole family joined in the worship of God. He gave generously to help the Jewish people,
3 and was regular in his prayers to God. One day about three in the afternoon he had a vision in which he clearly saw an angel of God, who came into his room and said,
4 'Cornelius!' He stared at him in terror. 'What is it, my lord?' he asked. The angel said, 'Your prayers and acts of charity have gone up to heaven to speak for you before
5 God. And now send to Joppa for a man named Simon,
6 also called Peter: he is lodging with another Simon, a
7 tanner, whose house is by the sea.' So when the angel who was speaking to him had gone, he summoned two

of his servants and a military orderly who was a religious
man, told them the whole story, and sent them to Joppa. 8

Next day, while they were still on their way and ap- 9
proaching the city, about noon Peter went up on the roof
to pray. He grew hungry and wanted something to eat. 10
While they were getting it ready, he fell into a trance.
He saw a rift in the sky, and a thing coming down that 11
looked like a great sheet of sail-cloth. It was slung by the
four corners, and was being lowered to the ground. In it 12
he saw creatures of every kind, whatever walks or crawls
or flies. Then there was a voice which said to him, 'Up, 13
Peter, kill and eat.' But Peter said, 'No, Lord, no: I have 14
never eaten anything profane or unclean.' The voice 15
came again a second time: 'It is not for you to call profane
what God counts clean.' This happened three times; and 16
then the thing was taken up again into the sky.

While Peter was still puzzling over the meaning of the 17
vision he had seen, the messengers of Cornelius had been
asking the way to Simon's house, and now arrived at the
entrance. They called out and asked if Simon Peter was 18
lodging there. But Peter was thinking over the vision, 19
when the Spirit said to him, 'Some men are here looking
for you; make haste and go downstairs. You may go with 20
them without any misgiving, for it was I who sent them.'
Peter came down to the men and said, 'You are looking 21
for me? Here I am. What brings you here?' 'We are 22
from the centurion Cornelius,' they replied, 'a good and
religious man, acknowledged as such by the whole Jewish
nation. He was directed by a holy angel to send for you
to his house and to listen to what you have to say.' So 23
Peter asked them in and gave them a night's lodging.

Next day he set out with them, accompanied by some members of the congregation at Joppa.

24 The day after that, he arrived at Caesarea. Cornelius was expecting them and had called together his relatives 25 and close friends. When Peter arrived, Cornelius came to meet him, and bowed to the ground in deep reverence. 26 But Peter raised him to his feet and said, 'Stand up; I am 27 a man like anyone else.' Still talking with him he went 28 in and found a large gathering. He said to them, 'I need not tell you that a Jew is forbidden by his religion to visit or associate with a man of another race; yet God has shown me clearly that I must not call any man profane 29 or unclean. That is why I came here without demur when you sent for me. May I ask what was your reason for sending?'

30 Cornelius said, 'Four days ago, just about this time, I was in the house here saying the afternoon prayers, when 31 suddenly a man in shining robes stood before me. He said: "Cornelius, your prayer has been heard and your 32 acts of charity remembered before God. Send to Joppa, then, to Simon Peter, and ask him to come. He is lodging 33 in the house of Simon the tanner, by the sea." So I sent to you there and then; it was kind of you to come. And now we are all met here before God, to hear all that the Lord has ordered you to say.'

34 Peter began: 'I now see how true it is that God has no 35 favourites, but that in every nation the man who is god-36 fearing and does what is right is acceptable to him. He sent his word to the Israelites and gave the good news of 37 peace through Jesus Christ, who is Lord of all. I need not tell you what happened lately all over the land of the

Jews, starting from Galilee after the baptism proclaimed
by John. You know about Jesus of Nazareth, how God 38
anointed him with the Holy Spirit and with power. He
went about doing good and healing all who were oppressed by the devil, for God was with him. And we can 39
bear witness to all that he did in the Jewish country-side
and in Jerusalem. He was put to death by hanging on a
gibbet; but God raised him to life on the third day, and 40
allowed him to appear, not to the whole people, but to 41
witnesses whom God had chosen in advance—to us, who
ate and drank with him after he rose from the dead. He 42
commanded us to proclaim him to the people, and affirm
that he is the one who has been designated by God as
judge of the living and the dead. It is to him that all the 43
prophets testify, declaring that everyone who trusts in
him receives forgiveness of sins through his name.'

Peter was still speaking when the Holy Spirit came 44
upon all who were listening to the message. The believers 45
who had come with Peter, men of Jewish birth, were
astonished that the gift of the Holy Spirit should have been
poured out even on Gentiles. For they could hear them 46
speaking in tongues of ecstasy and acclaiming the greatness
of God. Then Peter spoke: 'Is anyone prepared to with- 47
hold the water for baptism from these persons, who have
received the Holy Spirit just as we did ourselves?' Then 48
he ordered them to be baptized in the name of Jesus Christ.
After that they asked him to stay on with them for a time.

* The story of Peter and Cornelius makes it clear that the
Holy Spirit is about to claim the gentile world for his own.
It is, however, only a prelude to Paul's missionary work and
as such exceptional. Cornelius was not a proselyte, but he

was on the fringe of Judaism. *He gave generously to help the Jewish people, and was regular in his prayers to God* (10: 2). He was probably a 'God-fearer' like the eunuch in 8: 26–40 or like those in Pisidian Antioch whom Paul calls 'you who worship our God' (13: 16). Nevertheless, it is a remarkably important step that the leader of the apostles is taking and Luke so regards it.

1. *Caesarea*: a seaport, formerly Strato's Tower, built and renamed by Herod the Great. It was the Roman capital of the province of Judaea.

the Italian Cohort: an auxiliary unit, perhaps of freedmen.

3. The vision came in broad daylight at 3 p.m., the hour of prayer (cf. 3: 1) and Cornelius was terrified. The Holy Spirit spoke through a divine messenger—*an angel of God* (cf. 8: 26).

5–6. The instruction is precise, as befits one given to the commander of a century (the cohort would be divided into six centuries).

7–8. Cornelius sent two servants and a soldier, who like himself was *a religious man*, a 'God-fearer'.

9–16. Whilst they were on their way Peter also had a vision. He had gone to the roof-top at noon to pray. Once again, a great event in the history of the church begins with prayer (cf. 1: 24; 6: 6). While on the roof-top Peter grew hungry, and the vision may have been connected with his hunger. *He saw a rift in the sky* which meant a divine revelation was coming (cf. Stephen's theophany (appearance of God) in 7: 56). He was obviously thinking much of the gentile problem at this time and the clothful of animals, clean and unclean, lowered from the sky would give point to his thoughts. Jews would be represented by the clean, and Gentiles by the unclean animals.

11. *sail-cloth*: also a 'sheet', but the N.E.B. translation may well be right if Peter had been watching the boats in the harbour (Simon's house was *by the sea* (verse 6)) or if he was resting under an awning for protection against the noonday

sun. The mechanism of visions is often to be found in the way in which ordinary objects, having no significance in themselves, become the vehicles of a divine word (cf. Amos' basket of fruit, 8: 1–3; Jeremiah's almond-tree, 1: 11–12).

14. The laws relating to clean and unclean animals (Lev. 11) became specially important when Gentiles were admitted into the church, but God's command to eat cleansed all the animals in the sail-cloth.

16. The importance of the vision is emphasized by its three-fold appearance.

17–23. Meanwhile the deputation arrived and Peter's vision was made clear by the words: *You may go with them without any misgiving, for it was I who sent them.* The detail of the arrival of Cornelius' messengers, their night's stay and Peter's departure with them and *some members of the congregation at Joppa* are very vivid. It was vital that Luke's readers should understand the importance of what was happening and should see that every step was divinely controlled.

19. *Some men*: some manuscripts read 'two' (i.e. the servants); others, 'three' (including the soldier).

22. The brief character study of Cornelius by his own servants gives a good impression. Cf. the centurion at Capernaum whose servant Jesus healed (Luke 7: 4–5). The story in the Gospel was almost a preview of the coming of the Gentiles to Jesus, which is now the main subject of Luke's second book.

24–33. Doubtless Peter and his six companions (11: 12) learnt much from the three emissaries on the journey to Caesarea about the centurion and his friends. On their arrival Cornelius *bowed to the ground in deep reverence.* Cf. the attempted heathen worship of Barnabas and Paul by the people of Lystra, and the apostles' reply (14: 11–15). In the house Cornelius had collected *a large gathering* of relatives and friends. Peter went in at once explaining that God had shown him clearly *I must not call any man profane or unclean.*

The repetition of Cornelius' vision is an impressive sign to make the reader see the point. It is balanced by that of Peter in 11: 5–10. Similarly in 10: 28–9 the vision of Peter is referred to and this anticipates the drawing of the full consequences in 11: 11–18. It is a possible supposition that Philip's work in Caesarea (8: 40) had something to do with the considerable interest in Christianity there.

30. *a man in shining robes*: a divine messenger (cf. 'two men in dazzling garments' after the resurrection of Jesus, Luke 24: 4).

34–43. It is interesting to note the way in which Peter (like Paul later, e.g. at Lystra 14: 14–17; at Athens 17: 22–31) directs his words to his audience. Here he is dealing with an intelligent, far-seeing, informed group. It is a consummate summary of the gospel, from the baptism of Jesus to his resurrection, in half-a-dozen sentences. It had become clear to Peter from the events of the last few days that *God has no favourites*—neither individuals nor nations—*but that in every nation the man who is godfearing and does what is right is acceptable to him*. The purpose of the gospel was peace between God and man, and perhaps between Jew and Gentile through Jesus Christ, *who is Lord of all*, not of Jews only (cf. Rom. 2: 11 ff. 'For God has no favourites', etc.). Peter's hearers knew, perhaps from common knowledge in the province, perhaps from Philip's preaching (8: 40), the details of the Holy Spirit's work in Christ, and how Jesus was hanged on the cross and rose again, appearing to his own special witnesses. He is appointed *by God as judge of the living and the dead* (verse 42). The Old Testament prophets witnessed to his coming, and now that he has come, *everyone who trusts in him receives forgiveness of sins through his name*, whether Jew or Gentile.

41. A realistic emphasis on the resurrection body of Jesus—see the meals he ate with his witnesses, Luke 24: 30, 42–3; John 21: 9–13.

44–8. Peter's words to Cornelius and his friends are explanatory rather than missionary. The acts of his hearers had already proved their faith. There was no need of a confession; so the Holy Spirit acted with power before Peter had even

finished speaking. This was the gentile Pentecost, and is as vital
for the story in Acts as the Jewish Pentecost (2: 1–4). The Spirit
manifests himself in the same way—*for they could hear them
speaking in tongues of ecstasy and acclaiming the greatness of God.*
No wonder that Peter's Jewish companions were amazed. The
answer to Peter's question (verse 47) is obvious. If the Holy
Spirit has been given, of course Cornelius' party must be
admitted as members of the church through baptism.

45. *men of Jewish birth*: literally, 'of circumcision', but a
legitimate translation.

48. *in the name* (cf. 2: 38. Peter's advice after Pentecost),
as a sign that they were Jesus' possession, his servants.

stay on with them for a time: Peter did not withdraw from
them immediately. His vision had greatly affected him, if not
yet permanently (cf. Gal. 2: 11–12). ✻

PETER'S ACTION IS CONFIRMED

News came to the apostles and the members of the church **11**
in Judaea that Gentiles too had accepted the word of God;
and when Peter came up to Jerusalem those who were of 2
Jewish birth raised the question with him. 'You have been 3
visiting men who are uncircumcised,' they said, 'and sitting at table with them!' Peter began by laying before 4
them the facts as they had happened.

'I was in the city of Joppa', he said, 'at prayer; and 5
while in a trance I had a vision: a thing was coming down
that looked like a great sheet of sail-cloth, slung by the
four corners and lowered from the sky till it reached me.
I looked intently to make out what was in it and I saw 6
four-footed creatures of the earth, wild beasts, and things
that crawl or fly. Then I heard a voice saying to me, "Up, 7
Peter, kill and eat." But I said, "No, Lord, no: nothing 8
profane or unclean has ever entered my mouth." A voice 9

from heaven answered a second time, "It is not for you
10 to call profane what God counts clean." This happened
three times, and then they were all drawn up again into
11 the sky. At that moment three men, who had been sent
to me from Caesarea, arrived at the house where I was
12 staying; and the Spirit told me to go with them. My six
companions here came with me and we went into the
13 man's house. He told us how he had seen an angel
standing in his house who said, "Send to Joppa for Simon
14 also called Peter. He will speak words that will bring
15 salvation to you and all your household." Hardly had I
begun speaking, when the Holy Spirit came upon them,
16 just as upon us at the beginning. Then I recalled what the
Lord had said: "John baptized with water, but you will
17 be baptized with the Holy Spirit." God gave them no
less a gift than he gave us when we put our trust in the
Lord Jesus Christ; then how could I possibly stand in
God's way?'

18   When they heard this their doubts were silenced. They
gave praise to God and said, 'This means that God has
granted life-giving repentance to the Gentiles also.'

✻ Peter's action still needed confirmation by the church in
Jerusalem. This follows the same procedure as that in regard
to Philip's mission (8: 14–15), but its implications for the
future were much greater. It is significant that the apostles
needed so little persuasion to accept and approve Peter's
action. The church had advanced so steadily under the guidance
of the Holy Spirit from 'Jerusalem, and all over Judaea and
Samaria', that it was natural that it should now make a beginning on the final stage 'away to the ends of the earth' (1: 8).
The importance of the approval of the Jerusalem church in
the missionary work of the early church is further seen in

Barnabas' visit to Antioch (11: 22) and the meeting at Jerusalem (15: 1–35). It is worth noting in this discussion that no reference was made to Jesus' own condemnation of the Jewish food-law (Mark 7: 18–19).

1. *the apostles and the members of the church in Judaea*: the whole mother-church was involved, not merely the apostles.

2. *who were of Jewish birth*: literally 'of circumcision' (cf. 10: 45). Some manuscripts have a long introduction to this verse in which Peter appears to go on a long tour before eventually reaching Jerusalem, 'speaking at length and teaching them from district to district'. This makes Peter much more independent of the Jerusalem church, and may suggest the beginning of James' leadership there as a more orthodox Jew. The generally accepted text, as in the N.E.B., is more in line with Luke's plan of the church extending step by step, approved each time officially.

3. A similar charge was brought against Jesus. '"This fellow", they said, "welcomes sinners and eats with them"' (Luke 15: 2).

5–17. The repetition of the story indicates the importance which Luke accorded to it (cf. the conversion of Saul, 9: 1–30). He avoids using exactly the same phraseology, which gives a convincing freshness to the narrative.

11. *I was staying*: some manuscripts read 'we were', i.e. to include Peter's companions who accompanied him to Caesarea (10: 23). There is no earlier reference to any staying at Simon the tanner's (cf. 9: 43; 10: 6).

Some manuscripts also add to the sentence 'making no distinctions', i.e. between Jew and Gentile, or 'without any misgiving' as in 10: 20.

12. The first direct mention of Peter's *six companions* who have now gone up with him to Jerusalem as witnesses (cf. those who accompanied him from Joppa to Caesarea, 10: 23 and 45, to whom Cornelius spoke, 11: 13). They were hardly likely to have gone on the tour in the meanwhile with Peter, which makes the long insertion in verse 2 still more uncertain.

14. The angel's comment: *He will speak words that will bring salvation to you and all your household,* is an extension by Luke in the light of what had happened (cf. 10: 22).

15. The important point for Luke in Peter's report is the equation of what happened to the Gentiles at Caesarea with their own experience at Pentecost (2: 1–4).

16–17. Peter's recollection of Jesus' words (1: 5) is not mentioned earlier but it gives obvious weight to his argument. *God gave them no less a gift than he gave us when we put our trust in the Lord Jesus Christ.*

18. They were convinced that the Holy Spirit had guided Peter in this further extension of the church. The gospel of *life-giving repentance* was now available for Gentiles too. It is worth considering whether the Jerusalem church realized what it was doing. Luke knew what the outcome would eventually be. Perhaps in view of the later withdrawal from meals with gentile Christians of Peter, Barnabas and other Jewish believers (Gal. 2: 11–13) and the full-scale inquiry into Paul's work (15: 1–29), the approval given to Peter here was not meant to imply wholesale admission of Gentiles into the church. Nonetheless, it could have that interpretation and it was wise to hasten slowly.

The story of Peter from 9: 31 onwards is remarkably dramatic in form; each section is like a scene in a play and as such especially easy to memorize. It is a drama within the great drama of the developing church in Acts in which the Holy Spirit is the hero. In the scenes here Peter is to be found inexorably moving on through Lydda to Joppa and Caesarea to the climax in Cornelius' house, where to the amazement of them all the Spirit is given. Then the play moves in the last scene with purposeful finality to the free admission by the apostles of Gentiles into the church. *Their doubts were silenced,* so God be praised (11: 18). *

88

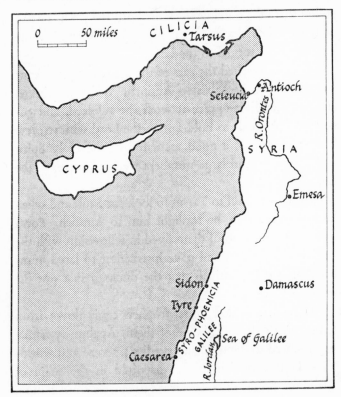

The church at Antioch

BARNABAS IN ANTIOCH IS JOINED BY SAUL

Meanwhile those who had been scattered after the per- 19
secution that arose over Stephen made their way to
Phoenicia, Cyprus, and Antioch, bringing the message to
Jews only and to no others. But there were some natives 20
of Cyprus and Cyrene among them, and these, when they
arrived at Antioch, began to speak to pagans as well,

21 telling them the good news of the Lord Jesus. The power of the Lord was with them, and a great many became believers, and turned to the Lord.

22 The news reached the ears of the church in Jerusalem;
23 and they sent Barnabas to Antioch. When he arrived and saw the divine grace at work, he rejoiced, and encouraged them all to hold fast to the Lord with resolute
24 hearts; for he was a good man, full of the Holy Spirit and of faith. And large numbers were won over to the Lord.

25, 26 He then went off to Tarsus to look for Saul; and when he had found him, he brought him to Antioch. For a whole year the two of them lived in fellowship with the congregation there, and gave instruction to large numbers. It was in Antioch that the disciples first got the name of Christians.

27 During this period some prophets came down from
28 Jerusalem to Antioch. One of them, Agabus by name, was inspired to stand up and predict a severe and worldwide famine, which in fact occurred in the reign of
29 Claudius. So the disciples agreed to make a contribution, each according to his means, for the relief of their fellow-
30 Christians in Judaea. This they did, and sent it off in the charge of Barnabas and Saul to the elders.

* During the first part of this section (verses 19–26) the church is found to be already established in Antioch in Syria. The account is linked with 8: 4 by reference to *those who had been scattered after the persecution that arose over Stephen.* They had apparently gone beyond Samaria to Phoenicia, the coastal plain between the Lebanon and the Mediterranean with its great ports of Tyre and Sidon which Paul visited later (21: 3;

27: 3); and also to Cyprus, which was the scene of Paul's first journey (13: 4–12); and finally to Antioch itself. It was a fine city, in size and importance the third in the Roman Empire. It stood on the Orontes in Syria and was earlier the capital of the Seleucid Empire, one of the three parts into which the empire of Alexander the Great broke up on his death. Herod the Great had recently embellished it by lining its principal street with columns. It was now the capital of the Roman legate (or viceroy) of the province of Syria and Cilicia, was a very cosmopolitan city and an excellent centre for the gentile church. The disciples from Jerusalem had brought *the message to Jews only and to no others* (verse 19), but soon after, some natives of Cyprus and Cyrene (like Barnabas (4: 36) and Lucius (13: 1)) began *to speak to pagans as well, telling them the good news of the Lord Jesus*. This time Barnabas was sent to take stock of the new extension and to approve it in the name of the Jerusalem church. When he saw the magnitude of the task in a mixed, Jewish-gentile community, he fetched Saul from Tarsus to help.

20. *pagans*: literally, 'Greeks'. Some manuscripts read 'Hellenists', i.e. Greek-speaking Jews, but clearly to make sense of the story Greeks is correct and the N.E.B. makes it clearer still by translating *pagans*. They may have been 'God-fearers', like Cornelius (10: 2), but there is no indication that they were. The missionaries were not official ministers; they probably passed on *the good news* as they went about their daily work. The same is probably true in other cities, e.g. Rome, where Paul found Christians who met him on his arrival (28: 15).

22–4. *Barnabas* (see 4: 36) was exactly the right person to go. The Jerusalem church knew their man. A Cypriot Jew was much more likely to be accepted than a Palestinian. His description resembles Stephen's (6: 5).

25–6. The selection of Saul as Barnabas' assistant is again a master-stroke. It was Barnabas who had 'introduced him to the apostles' (9: 27) when the disciples in Jerusalem were apprehensive. Now they worked together amicably (cf. 15: 39) for a year living *in fellowship with the congregation.*

There is no indication here of how long Saul had been in Tarsus. Gal. 2: 1 speaks of 14 years before Saul and Barnabas went up to Jerusalem again, which was probably the visit in connexion with the collection for those in need through the famine (11: 30). It seems more reasonable to equate the visit mentioned in Gal. 2: 1 with this famine-visit than with that to the council in Acts 15: 2. (See note on p. 75 on the different emphases placed by Paul and Luke on these chronological details.)

26. *Christians*: probably a name given by the people of Antioch to distinguish them from the Jews, though there is no indication that the name was given at this time. Some have thought it a nickname but it is in line with similar nouns (e.g. Herodians, Matt. 22: 16, R.V., R.S.V.), i.e. of Christ's party (cf. 'of Herod's party', Matt. 22: 16, N.E.B.).

27–30. The arrival of the prophets from Jerusalem led to Agabus' prediction of famine and the visit of Barnabas and Saul to Judaea with relief.

27. *prophets*: they were well known in the early church as inspired speakers (e.g. Judas and Silas, 15: 32; Philip's daughters, 21: 9). Paul felt the need for their organization in Corinth (1 Cor. 14: 29) and in Thessalonica (1 Thess. 5: 19–22). They are placed second after 'apostles' in the list of those to whom the divine gifts were made (1 Cor. 12: 28; Eph. 4: 11). Outside the New Testament they seem to have become wandering preachers and tests were devised to distinguish between true and false.

28. *Agabus* also prophesied Paul's arrest in Jerusalem (21: 10–11). An alternative reading introduces at this point the first 'we-section' (see above, p. 3): 'And there was much rejoicing; and when we were assembled together one of them, Agabus by name, spoke...' It is likely that this addition to the text arose from the tradition that Luke came from Antioch and thus a scribe assumed his presence on this occasion. Alternatively, confusion might have arisen between Luke's

name and that of Lucius of Cyrene mentioned as one of the
company at Antioch in 13: 1.

Claudius: the inference is that the prophecy took place
before the reign of the Emperor Claudius (A.D. 41–54) and
that it was fulfilled in it. The Roman historians Tacitus and
Suetonius both refer to famines in Claudius' reign. Josephus
(*Antiquities* XX. 5. 2) says 'that great famine happened in Judaea'
about A.D. 46. It was obviously serious from the use of the
phrase world-wide (also used in Luke 2: 1 for the registration,
where the N.E.B. paraphrases 'Roman world'), though presumably it did not reach Antioch.

29. *The relief* sent to Christians in Judaea emphasizes the
unity of the church, whether Jew or gentile, and the loyalty
to the mother-church in Jerusalem. There is no direct reference
in Acts (24: 17 may suggest it) to the collection for the church
in Jerusalem which Paul regarded as so important (2 Cor. 9).

30. *Barnabas and Saul* are sent as ambassadors to *the elders*
in Jerusalem. With James as the president, the apostles and
elders were the governing body of the church in Jerusalem
(15: 6, 23). Later when the apostles, and presumably the
Seven, had left the city, the elders would remain in control.
They may have modelled their organization on the synagogue
system, and the pattern in Jerusalem may well have served
for later developments, e.g. in Lystra, Iconium and Pisidian
Antioch, where Paul and Barnabas 'appointed elders for them
in each congregation' (14: 23). ✳

PETER AND HEROD

It was about this time that King Herod attacked certain **12**
members of the church. He beheaded James, the brother 2
of John, and then, when he saw that the Jews approved, 3
proceeded to arrest Peter also. This happened during the
festival of Unleavened Bread. Having secured him, he 4
put him in prison under a military guard, four squads of

four men each, meaning to produce him in public after
5 Passover. So Peter was kept in prison under constant watch,
while the church kept praying fervently for him to God.

6   On the very night before Herod had planned to bring
him forward, Peter was asleep between two soldiers,
secured by two chains, while outside the doors sentries
7 kept guard over the prison. All at once an angel of the
Lord stood there, and the cell was ablaze with light. He
tapped Peter on the shoulder and woke him. 'Quick!
Get up', he said, and the chains fell away from his wrists.
8 The angel then said to him, 'Do up your belt and put
your shoes on.' He did so. 'Now wrap your cloak round
9 you and follow me.' He followed him out, with no idea
that the angel's intervention was real: he thought it was
10 just a vision. But they passed the first guard-post, then
the second, and reached the iron gate leading out into the
city, which opened for them of its own accord. And so
they came out and walked the length of one street; and
the angel left him.

11   Then Peter came to himself. 'Now I know it is true,'
he said; 'the Lord has sent his angel and rescued me from
Herod's clutches and from all that the Jewish people were
12 expecting.' When he realized how things stood, he made
for the house of Mary, the mother of John Mark, where
13 a large company was at prayer. He knocked at the outer
14 door and a maid called Rhoda came to answer it. She
recognized Peter's voice and was so overjoyed that instead
of opening the door she ran in and announced that Peter
15 was standing outside. 'You are crazy', they told her; but
she insisted that it was so. Then they said, 'It must be his
guardian angel.'

Meanwhile Peter went on knocking, and when they 16
opened the door and saw him, they were astounded. With 17
a movement of the hand he signed to them to keep quiet,
and told them how the Lord had brought him out of
prison. 'Report this to James and the members of the
church', he said. Then he left the house and went off
elsewhere.

When the morning came, there was consternation 18
among the soldiers: what could have become of Peter?
Herod made close search, but failed to find him, so he 19
interrogated the guards and ordered their execution.

Afterwards he left Judaea to reside for a time at Caesarea. He had for some time been furiously angry with 20
the people of Tyre and Sidon, who now by common
agreement presented themselves at his court. There they
won over Blastus the royal chamberlain, and sued for
peace, because their country drew its supplies from the
king's territory. So, on an appointed day, attired in his 21
royal robes and seated on the rostrum, Herod harangued
them; and the populace shouted back, 'It is a god 22
speaking, not a man!' Instantly an angel of the Lord 23
struck him down, because he had usurped the honour due
to God; he was eaten up with worms and died.

Meanwhile the word of God continued to grow and 24
spread.

Barnabas and Saul, their task fulfilled, returned from 25
Jerusalem, taking John Mark with them.

☆ This is another incident full of dramatic power. Apart from his witness at the council in Jerusalem (15: 6–11), this is Peter's last appearance in the drama of the Spirit that Luke is writing. The contrast between Peter and Herod is marked.

The apostle escapes from the clutches of the king guided by *an angel of the Lord* (verse 7). *'Now I know it is true,'* he said; *'the Lord has sent his angel and rescued me from Herod's clutches and from all that the Jewish people were expecting'* (verse 11). Despite his search, Herod failed to find Peter, and before long, for his blasphemy in accepting the worship of the populace (verse 22), *an angel of the Lord struck him down, because he had usurped the honour due to God* (verse 23), and *the word of God continued to grow and spread* (verse 24). Cf. the same dramatic comparison between Barnabas and Ananias and Sapphira (4: 36 — 5: 12).

1. *King Herod*: Herod Agrippa I (died A.D. 44), grandson of Herod the Great; educated in Rome where he secured the favour of the emperors Caligula and Claudius. From them he received the former tetrarchies of Lysanias and Philip, then the district of Galilee, formerly ruled by Herod Antipas (Luke 3: 1), and lastly Judaea and Samaria. This made him king of a considerable area, and his persecution of the church may well have been an attempt to win favour with the Jews.

2. *James, the brother of John*: the reference to the execution of James seems callously brief, as he had occupied such a special place with Peter and John in the Gospel story (e.g. at the raising of Jairus' daughter, Luke 8: 51; at the transfiguration, Luke 9: 28). The Jewish approval of James' death encouraged Herod to arrest Peter (verse 3). The account of his imprisonment is the last story about Peter in Acts before he is superseded by Paul. The tradition, originating with Papias (*c.* 60–130), bishop of Hierapolis in Asia Minor, that John was put to death with James in fulfilment of Jesus' prophecy: 'the cup that I drink you shall drink' (Mark 10: 39), seems unlikely or Luke would surely have mentioned it.

3. *the festival of Unleavened Bread*: the Passover (Luke 22: 1).

4. *a military guard*: a strong one, *four squads of four men each*, if all on duty together. It gives some indication of the strength of feeling on the side of the apostles. Perhaps Herod anticipated a release such as that in 5: 17–21. The time of the arrest

and the plan *to produce him in public after Passover*, presumably to avoid bloodshed on a holy day, recall the crucifixion of Jesus.

5. Luke's emphasis on prayer is again apparent (cf. 1: 24-5; 6: 6).

6-10. The story of the release is full of dramatic reality. Peter is certainly not planning an escape and his friends are praying, not plotting. The angelic instructions are precise and the detail of the escape is most convincing. Peter's own comment is obviously Luke's; 'Now I know it is true' (verse 11). The story should be compared with the imprisonment and release of the apostles (5: 17-21) and of Paul and Silas (16: 19-34).

10. Some manuscripts add 'and went down the seven steps' after *came out*. This may be a piece of genuine knowledge, or possibly a reference to the seven steps into the Temple according to Ezekiel's description (40: 22, 26). This might be more likely if the prison was in the fortress of Antonia (built by Herod the Great and named in honour of Mark Antony), north-west of the Temple.

12. *the house of Mary, the mother of John Mark*: it must have been a house of considerable size, for there was *a large company ...at prayer* there. Although there is no real evidence for the identification, it is natural to imagine that this was the same meeting-place where Jesus and the apostles assembled for the Last Supper (Luke 22: 7-13) and where the disciples met before Pentecost (1: 12-14; 2: 1-4). James (the Lord's brother) and other church leaders were apparently not present (verse 17).

John Mark: introduced because of the part he is to play later with Barnabas and Paul (13: 5). He was a relative of Barnabas (Col. 4: 10) and later accompanied him to Cyprus (15: 39) after Barnabas separated from Paul on his account. His friendship with Paul was later re-established: 'Pick up Mark and bring him with you' (2 Tim. 4: 11); 'Mark, Aristarchus, Demas, and Luke, my fellow-workers' (Philem. 24). His friendship with Peter is obvious from the reference to 'my son Mark' in 1 Pet. 5: 13 and it may well be that he is the Mark who, according to Papias, wrote the second gospel as 'Peter's interpreter'.

13. *Rhoda*: another very personal touch. Her thrill at Peter's presence says much for her and for him.

15. *his guardian angel*: literally, 'his angel'. The idea of a spiritual guardian had developed in post-exilic times, perhaps under the Persian influence. 'A good angel shall go with him, and his journey shall be prospered' (Tobit 5: 21). Jesus says 'of these little ones; I tell you, they have their guardian angels in heaven' (Matt. 18: 10). The author of Hebrews refers to angels as 'ministrant spirits, sent out to serve, for the sake of those who are to inherit salvation' (1: 14).

17. *James*, 'the Lord's brother' (Gal. 1: 19) was already becoming the leader of the Jerusalem church in succession to Peter and is associated with 'Cephas and John' as 'those reputed pillars of our society' (Gal. 2: 9). He was presumably the James of Mark 6: 3, one of the family at Nazareth.

Where did Peter go? The literal meaning 'to another place' is interpreted *elsewhere* in the N.E.B. and is probably right. He seems to have left Jerusalem on his own missionary travels (e.g. Antioch (Gal. 2: 11); Corinth (1 Cor. 1: 12)).

19. *ordered their execution*: literally, 'ordered them to be led away', to which some manuscripts add 'to be killed'.

20. The trouble between Herod and Tyre and Sidon was probably economic, since the two cities depended on corn from Galilee. A personal touch is again introduced by the intrigue with *Blastus the royal chamberlain*.

21-3. Herod's death is plainly interpreted by Luke as a divine punishment for blasphemy in accepting *the honour due to God*. Josephus (*Antiquities* XIX. 8. 2) tells another story quite different from Luke's. Herod was celebrating a show in honour of the emperor and on the second day he appeared in a garment made wholly of silver which glittered in the sunlight so that his friends started the cry that he was a god. Then he saw an owl sitting on a rope, which he took to be an evil omen, and he was seized with pain in the belly and died five days later. After Herod's death (A.D. 44) Palestine became a Roman province.

24. The church continued to grow despite efforts like Herod's to check it. This brief note indicates the power of the Spirit in the spread of the church, no matter how men raved against it.

25. The interlude is over and the account reverts to Barnabas and Saul (11: 30). Some manuscripts read '*to* Jerusalem', which seems strange unless it is read with *their task*, i.e. 'their task to Jerusalem fulfilled, returned taking John Mark with them'. The reference to Mark leads onwards to his part with Barnabas and Saul on their first journey. ✳

The Church Breaks Barriers

FIRST, IN CYPRUS

THERE WERE at Antioch, in the congregation there, **13** certain prophets and teachers: Barnabas, Simeon called Niger, Lucius of Cyrene, Manaen, who had been at the court of Prince Herod, and Saul. While they were 2 keeping a fast and offering worship to the Lord, the Holy Spirit said, 'Set Barnabas and Saul apart for me, to do the work to which I have called them.' Then, after further 3 fasting and prayer, they laid their hands on them and let them go.

So these two, sent out on their mission by the Holy 4 Spirit, came down to Seleucia, and from there sailed to Cyprus. Arriving at Salamis, they declared the word of 5 God in the Jewish synagogues. They had John with them

6 as their assistant. They went through the whole island as far as Paphos, and there they came upon a sorcerer, a Jew
7 who posed as a prophet, Bar-Jesus by name. He was in the retinue of the Governor, Sergius Paulus, an intelligent man, who had sent for Barnabas and Saul and wanted to
8 hear the word of God. This Elymas the sorcerer (so his name may be translated) opposed them, trying to turn
9 the Governor away from the Faith. But Saul, also known as Paul, filled with the Holy Spirit, looked him in the face
10 and said, 'You utter impostor and charlatan! You son of the devil and enemy of all goodness, will you never stop
11 falsifying the straight ways of the Lord? Look now, the hand of the Lord strikes: you shall be blind, and for a time you shall not see the sunlight.' Instantly mist and darkness came over him and he groped about for someone to
12 lead him by the hand. When the Governor saw what had happened he became a believer, deeply impressed by what he learned about the Lord.

* Antioch is the new centre of the church. There is a steady radiation of missionary effort from there, until by the end of Acts the church has reached Rome. The momentum of Luke's story, which is the momentum of the Holy Spirit himself, steadily increases as town after town, people after people, hear the word of the Lord. Thus the account is full of bustling interest; believers and unbelievers jostle each other; Jews and Gentiles eventually find a common place together in the church; and behind it all is the dynamic power of the Spirit, showing the Way.

The group in 13: 1 reads like an executive committee with whom rested decisions on future policy. *Prophets and teachers* are listed by Paul as following apostles in the community. They were clearly men inspired by the Spirit for his work and as such they waited upon him with fasting and worship and prayer (verses 2 and 3).

1. As usual Luke introduces new characters without preliminary comment. They are Simeon Niger (perhaps from central Africa, where the eunuch lived, 8: 27), Lucius from Cyrene (the country of Simon, Luke 23: 26; cf. also Acts 11: 20), Manaen, a companion of Herod Antipas, and, one feels Luke saying, Barnabas and Saul, whom you have met before. Manaen (Hebrew: *Menahem*) was (literally) 'brought up with' Herod as a 'foster-brother' and so became a companion at his court. Prince Herod, literally Herod the tetrarch (of Galilee), was Herod Antipas, Luke 3: 1.

2. The Holy Spirit is the source of all direction in the church and to the waiting committee he speaks (through one of them). The setting, as usual in a great moment in the church's development, is one of prayer. This time *a fast* is added to it, as if waiting for the absent Lord to make his will known (Luke 5: 35).

offering worship: literally, 'performing service' or, as in Athens, 'a liturgy', a burdensome public duty.

Set Barnabas and Saul apart for me: 'Separate' (R.V.)—used by Moses in speaking to Korah with reference to the Levites who became the priestly caste (Num. 16: 9), and in 1 Chron. 23: 13 of Aaron, 'that he should sanctify the most holy things'. Paul himself uses the word for his own call (Rom. 1: 1, 'set apart for the service of the Gospel'; Gal. 1: 15, 'God, who had set me apart from birth').

3. *they laid their hands on them*: an act of commissioning, closely associating them with the church in Antioch that is sending them, and of blessing for the work.

and let them go: a better translation than 'sent them away' (R.V.).

4. Further emphasis on the Holy Spirit as directing the way for them to go.

Seleucia: the port of Antioch at the mouth of the Orontes, 16 miles away.

Cyprus: chosen for the first stage, probably because it was Barnabas' home (4: 36).

5. *Salamis*: the eastern port on the island, where they would naturally land. Its ruins are north of the modern Famagusta. As usual, the work began in the synagogues. There was a large Jewish population in Cyprus. John Mark's position as *assistant*

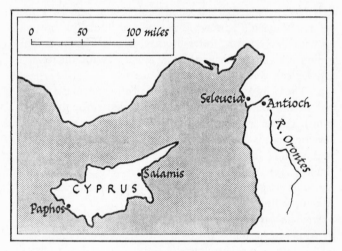

Paul in Cyprus

may well have been that of an apprentice, doing the menial tasks while learning the main job.

6–8. *They went through the whole island* i.e. from north-east to south-west. The impression is not merely of a straightforward journey but of work by the way. There had been some sort of mission to Cyprus before (11: 19).

Paphos: the capital of the island and seat of the Roman governor.

a sorcerer, a Jew who posed as a prophet, Bar-Jesus by name: the story of this encounter with sorcery resembles Peter's contest with Simon in Samaria (8: 18–24). This Jew, who must have claimed some sort of inspiration as a prophet, was *in the retinue of the Governor*, as his astrologer or magus (the same word is used for the 'astrologers' in Matt. 2: 1 who came 'from the east' at Jesus' birth). His name, *Bar-Jesus*, must have sounded particularly unpleasant to the apostles and hence is probably correct. *Elymas* is not the equivalent of Bar-Jesus, which makes the parenthesis (*so his name may be translated*) difficult to explain. The main suggestions are that the alternative reading for Elymas in some manuscripts, 'Hetoimas', which may be translated 'ready', is from the same root as Bar-Jesus, or that Elymas is a translation of 'sorcerer' and represents the Arabic for 'wise'. This latter might point to a link with 'the astrologers (magi) from the east' (Matt. 2: 1).

the Governor, Sergius Paulus: the title in Greek is the equivalent of the Latin, proconsul. Cyprus had been made a senatorial province by Augustus in 22 B.C. and would be governed by a propraetor (called here by courtesy 'a proconsul').

9. Now that the Christian church is moving away from Palestine into the more gentile world, Saul would normally use his Roman name Paulus. Perhaps Luke was reminded of this by the Governor's name.

There is no article in Greek before *Holy Spirit*, which makes the phrase even more potent, i.e. divine power.

10-12. This denunciation throws light on Paul's character. There is a suppressed fury in it that makes the charge quite terrifying.

utter impostor and charlatan: literally, 'full of all wickedness and recklessness'. Bar-Jesus had interposed his own devilish designs between the Governor and *the straight ways of the Lord*. Retribution was bound to fall. The effect of the divine word is always judgement when it meets with evil (cf. John 3: 18). Paul himself knew well the horror of the darkness, when *he groped about for someone to lead him by the hand* (cf. 9: 8). The blindness was obviously temporary—*for a time you shall not see the sunlight*—so perhaps at the end of it he, like the Governor, *became a believer*.

For Luke, this brief but vividly dramatic scene has the two-fold purpose of showing the futility of attempting to prevent the way of the Spirit, and of pointing to the conflict which would now become more apparent between Judaism and the church. ✳

The advance into Asia Minor

THE OTHER ANTIOCH

Leaving Paphos, Paul and his companions went by sea to Perga in Pamphylia; John, however, left them and returned to Jerusalem. From Perga they continued their journey as far as Pisidian Antioch. On the Sabbath they

went to synagogue and took their seats; and after the 15
readings from the Law and the prophets, the officials of
the synagogue sent this message to them: 'Friends, if you
have anything to say to the people by way of exhortation,
let us hear it.' Paul rose, made a gesture with his hand, 16
and began:

'Men of Israel and you who worship our God, listen
to me! The God of this people of Israel chose our fathers. 17
When they were still living as aliens in Egypt he made
them into a nation and brought them out of that country
with arm outstretched. For some forty years he bore with 18
their conduct in the desert. Then in the Canaanite country 19
he overthrew seven nations, whose lands he gave them to
be their heritage for some four hundred and fifty years, 20
and afterwards appointed judges for them until the time
of the prophet Samuel.

'Then they asked for a king and God gave them Saul 21
the son of Kish, a man of the tribe of Benjamin, who
reigned for forty years. Then he removed him and set up 22
David as their king, giving him his approval in these words:
"I have found David son of Jesse to be a man after my own
heart, who will carry out all my purposes." This is the man 23
from whose posterity God, as he promised, has brought
Israel a saviour, Jesus. John made ready for his coming by 24
proclaiming baptism as a token of repentance to the whole
people of Israel. And when John was nearing the end of 25
his course, he said, "I am not what you think I am. No,
after me comes one whose shoes I am not fit to unfasten."

'My brothers, you who come of the stock of Abraham, 26
and others among you who revere our God, we are the
people to whom the message of this salvation has been

27 sent. The people of Jerusalem and their rulers did not recognize him, or understand the words of the prophets which are read Sabbath by Sabbath; indeed they fulfilled 28 them by condemning him. Though they failed to find grounds for the sentence of death, they asked Pilate to 29 have him executed. And when they had carried out all that the scriptures said about him, they took him down 30 from the gibbet and laid him in a tomb. But God raised 31 him from the dead; and there was a period of many days during which he appeared to those who had come up with him from Galilee to Jerusalem.

32 'They are now his witnesses before our nation; and we are here to give you the good news that God, who made 33 the promise to the fathers, has fulfilled it for the children by raising Jesus from the dead, as indeed it stands written, in the second Psalm: "You are my son; this day have 34 I begotten you." Again, that he raised him from the dead, never again to revert to corruption, he declares in these words: "I will give you the blessings promised to David, 35 holy and sure." This is borne out by another passage: "Thou wilt not let thy loyal servant suffer corruption." 36 As for David, when he had served the purpose of God in his own generation, he died, and was gathered to his 37 fathers, and suffered corruption; but the one whom God 38 raised up did not suffer corruption; and you must understand, my brothers, that it is through him that forgiveness 39 of sins is now being proclaimed to you. It is through him that everyone who has faith is acquitted of everything for which there was no acquittal under the Law of Moses. 40 Beware, then, lest you bring down upon yourselves the 41 doom proclaimed by the prophets: "See this, you scoffers,

wonder, and begone; for I am doing a deed in your days, a deed which you will never believe when you are told of it."'

As they were leaving the synagogue they were asked 42 to come again and speak on these subjects next Sabbath; and after the congregation had dispersed, many Jews and 43 gentile worshippers went along with Paul and Barnabas, who spoke to them and urged them to hold fast to the grace of God.

On the following Sabbath almost the whole city ga- 44 thered to hear the word of God. When the Jews saw the 45 crowds, they were filled with jealous resentment, and contradicted what Paul and Barnabas said, with violent abuse. But Paul and Barnabas were outspoken in their 46 reply. 'It was necessary', they said, 'that the word of God should be declared to you first. But since you reject it and thus condemn yourselves as unworthy of eternal life, we now turn to the Gentiles. For these are our in- 47 structions from the Lord: "I have appointed you to be a light for the Gentiles, and a means of salvation to earth's farthest bounds."' When the Gentiles heard this, they 48 were overjoyed and thankfully acclaimed the word of the Lord, and those who were marked out for eternal life became believers. So the word of the Lord spread far and 49 wide through the region. But the Jews stirred up feeling 50 among the women of standing who were worshippers, and among the leading men of the city; a persecution was started against Paul and Barnabas, and they were expelled from the district. So they shook the dust off their feet in 51 protest against them and went to Iconium. And the con- 52 verts were filled with joy and with the Holy Spirit.

* The vital sentence in this passage is *we now turn to the Gentiles* (verse 46). It is no wonder that Luke dwells at length on the events which led up to this momentous statement. The Holy Spirit had progressed far during this journey of his apostles and a great new future opened for the church. There was no doubt that the commissioning committee in Antioch in Syria would approve (14: 27), but would the governing body in Jerusalem (15: 4-5)?

13. Paul now becomes the leader of the party (cf. 9: 15) despite the seniority of Barnabas.

Perga is on the river Cestrus, eight miles from the sea. Its port is Attalia.

It is impossible to determine the reason for Mark's return to Jerusalem. Paul regarded it as a desertion of the cause (15: 38) but it says something for Mark that he had the courage of his convictions, and returned. This perhaps implies that he did not approve either of Paul's plan for work in Asia Minor, or of his very probable approach to Gentiles, or even of his methods (cf. with Elymas, verses 9-11).

14. *Pisidian Antioch*: not actually in Pisidia but near the Pisidian border. It was founded by Seleucus Nicator. It was a Roman colony and the chief city in the district of Phrygia in the Roman province of Galatia.

15. The Sabbath service in the synagogue resembles that which Jesus attended in Nazareth (Luke 4: 16 ff.). *After the readings from the Law and the prophets, the officials of the synagogue* invited them to speak. The officials (literally, 'rulers') were presumably leading members of the synagogue; the president who was responsible for the service was usually known as 'the ruler of the synagogue'. Paul as a Pharisee and Barnabas as a Levite would obviously be the kind of people to be invited.

16-41. Paul rises to address his hearers with a rhetorical flourish of the hand. He calls them *men of Israel and you who worship our God*, i.e. gentile 'God-fearers' like Cornelius and his household (10: 2). There is a general resemblance between

Paul's address and those of Peter (chapters 2 and 3) and Stephen (chapter 7). Throughout Israel's history God has in mind the coming of the Messiah, and the work of the patriarchs, kings and prophets is a preparation for it. Then, immediately before Jesus came, John the Baptist announced the saviour of Israel. Despite the teaching of the prophets, which was read to them every week, the Jews of Jerusalem *did not recognize him* (verse 27) and so fulfilled the scriptures by having him crucified. *But God raised him from the dead* (verse 30). This is the good news we bring you, and it is through this Jesus that *forgiveness of sins is now being proclaimed to you* (verse 38). What the Law of Moses could not do, faith in Jesus can. (See note on the speeches in Acts on pp. 30–1.)

17. Paul begins with the choice of Israel for God's purpose, and at once refers to her redemption from Egypt, as a symbol of the redemption from the bondage of sin brought about by Jesus.

18. *bore with their conduct*: some manuscripts have a better variant, 'sustained them'. The meaning is the same as in Deut. 1: 31, 'the Lord thy God bare thee, as a man doth bear his son'.

19. *overthrew seven nations*: according to Deut. 7: 1 'the Hittite, and the Girgashite, and the Amorite, and the Canaanite, and the Perizzite, and the Hivite, and the Jebusite, seven nations greater and mightier than thou'.

some four hundred and fifty years: one manuscript assumes this to be the period of the Judges; but most, as the N.E.B. translation implies, regard it as the period from the beginning of exile in Egypt to the end of the conquest of Canaan. 1 Kings 6: 1 refers to a longer period of 480 years 'after the children of Israel were come out of the land of Egypt, in the fourth year of Solomon's reign'.

20. *Samuel*: is considered the first prophet, as in Peter's speech (3: 24).

21. The length of Saul's reign is not given in the Old Testament, but Josephus (*Antiquities* VI. 14. 9) also gives the conventional period of 40 years.

22. Just as David replaced Saul, so his descendant, Jesus, has replaced the teaching of the old Israel with his own. The quotation is a combination of Ps. 89: 20—'I have found David'—and 1 Sam. 13: 14—'a man after his own heart' with a reference to the description of Cyrus in Isa. 44: 28, who 'shall perform all my pleasure'.

24. John's baptism was a prelude to the coming of the Messiah and the end of the pre-Christian revelation addressed as it was *to the whole people of Israel* (cf. Luke 3: 3).

25. When the people wondered whether John himself was the Messiah he pointed to the one who should come after him (Luke 3: 15–16). For Luke, John was the vital link between the old and the new. 'Until John, it was the Law and the prophets: since then, there is the good news of the kingdom of God' (Luke 16: 16).

26. A repetition of his opening address to Jews and 'God-fearers'.

27–31. A very concise statement of the essential elements in the crucifixion and resurrection of Jesus: the Jerusalem Jews failed to recognize him, though they heard the prophecies about him every Sabbath; they condemned him and sought his execution, though they had no valid grounds; his death fulfilled the scriptures, and then God raised him up, as his disciples witnessed. Despite this summary it must be remembered that some Jerusalem Jews, even including priests, had subsequently joined the church (6: 7 and note on 3: 11–26).

32. Paul does not include his own vision (9: 3–6) as witness of the resurrection to an audience such as this, though he did so later in writing to the Corinthians (1 Cor. 15: 8–9). He was giving a normal early Christian sermon and such a detail would be out of place.

33. *the children*: some manuscripts read 'our children', as R.V.; others 'us their children', as R.S.V. The good news promised to the fathers has been given to the children through the resurrection of Jesus from the dead. Ps. 2: 7 is used as the proof-text of the event. Some manuscripts read 'first' Psalm,

as some Hebrew manuscripts combine Psalms 1 and 2, but it is also possible that the first psalm was regarded as an introductory blessing to the whole Psalter, just as Psalm 150 was regarded as a closing doxology.

34. Prophetic support for the messianic resurrection is found in Isa. 55: 3.

35. *This is borne out*: the reference is to Ps. 16: 10, a regular proof-text for the resurrection and used by Peter after Pentecost (2: 27).

36–8. This text obviously cannot refer to David, for he died; but the Messiah was raised up by God and *it is through him that forgiveness of sins is now being proclaimed to you* (see above on 1: 15–20 for note on the early Christian use of 'proof-texts').

39. *is acquitted*: literally, 'is justified' or 'is set right'. The idea seems to be that faith will set a man right beyond those things for which the Law will set him right. This is not the Pauline doctrine whereby faith takes the place of any kind of legalistic approach, but there is a clear indication that faith goes beyond *the Law of Moses*.

40–1. He concludes with the warning from Hab. 1: 5 of what will happen to those who refuse to understand the work of the Messiah.

42–3. Paul has certainly impressed his hearers and though the orthodox were doubtless suspicious (see verse 45) many wanted to hear more (cf. the similar reaction of a very different audience in Athens, 17: 32). Indeed, *many Jews and gentile worshippers* (Greek: 'proselytes', but 'God-fearers' rather than converts to Judaism) followed Paul and Barnabas after the service, perhaps to their lodgings (cf. Paul in Rome, 28: 23), where the missionaries urged them to remain firm in the knowledge of the faith (*grace*) that they had now been given by God.

44–9. Rumour had obviously been busy throughout the week and one can hardly assume that Paul and Barnabas had been inactive. The result was that on the next Sabbath an enormous crowd of all sorts of people met *to hear the word of God*. There is no mention of a synagogue service and in view of the size of the crowd—*almost the whole city*—it is likely that the meeting took place elsewhere. The Jews, presumably the authorities of the synagogue and the orthodox members, aroused to jealous fury, contradicted and violently abused the missionaries. They were probably alarmed at Paul's challenge to the Law and at the presence of Gentiles in the crowd as well as Jews and 'God-fearers'. The reply of Paul and Barnabas is the theme-song of Acts. *The word of God must be declared to you* (Jews) *first. But since you reject it and thus condemn yourselves as unworthy of eternal life, we now turn to the Gentiles* (cf. 18: 6, at Corinth; 22: 21, in Jerusalem; 26: 20, in Caesarea; 28: 28, in Rome).

47. Israel herself should have been *a light for the Gentiles* (Isa. 49: 6) but since she has rejected the Messiah, who himself was 'A light that will be a revelation to the heathen' (Luke 2: 32), his servants will take the message *to earth's farthest bounds*, as Christ commissioned them in 1: 8. In Rom. 11: 25–32 Paul makes it clear that to him the fullness of the work of the church can only come when all men—Jews and Gentiles—are drawn into the salvation of Christ.

48. The joy that followed the Way from the first days of the church (2: 46) now spread to the Gentiles of Pisidian Antioch.

marked out for eternal life: the N.E.B. avoids the suggestion of predestination, which 'ordained' (R.V. and R.S.V.) might imply. They were marked out for the resurrection life in Christ because they accepted the good news. The result was the rapid spread of the word throughout the region.

50. Meanwhile the Jews were hard at work among the influential women of the city, who held a higher position in Asia Minor than in other parts of the empire. They probably influenced their husbands, the city magistrates, to expel the missionaries, though it could not have been a permanent expulsion as they were back before long.

51. *shook the dust off their feet*, as Jesus had commanded (Luke 9: 5) 'as a warning to them'.

Iconium: a town about 80 miles south-east of Antioch on the borders of Phrygia and Lycaonia in the province of Galatia.

52. The Spirit had triumphed in this tremendous move forward. It was indeed a time of rejoicing.

Luke's picture of life in Pisidian Antioch is just sufficient to give the reader an idea of what it was like—the flourishing synagogue, with its well-read members in a predominantly gentile town, the natural inquisitiveness of the populace, the abusive jealousy of the synagogue rulers, the mob enthusiasm, the influential women and the city magistrates; and into the midst of it all the Holy Spirit thrusts Paul and Barnabas. This vivid sketching will be repeated many times in the rest of Acts. Luke is thrilled by the story he is telling of his great hero, and rejoices to recall him at his task. ✻

JUPITER AND MERCURY!

At Iconium similarly they went into the Jewish synagogue **14** and spoke to such purpose that a large body both of Jews and Greeks became believers. But the unconverted Jews 2 stirred up the Gentiles and poisoned their minds against the Christians. For some time Paul and Barnabas stayed 3 on and spoke boldly and openly in reliance on the Lord; and he confirmed the message of his grace by causing signs and miracles to be worked at their hands. The mass 4 of the townspeople were divided, some siding with the Jews, others with the apostles. But when a move was 5 made by Gentiles and Jews together, with the connivance of the city authorities, to maltreat them and stone them, they got wind of it and made their escape to the Lycaonian 6 cities of Lystra and Derbe and the surrounding country, where they continued to spread the good news. 7

8 At Lystra sat a crippled man, lame from birth, who had
9 never walked in his life. This man listened while Paul was
speaking. Paul looked him in the face and saw that he
10 had the faith to be cured, so he said to him in a loud voice,
'Stand up straight on your feet'; and he sprang up and
11 started to walk. When the crowds saw what Paul had
done, they shouted, in their native Lycaonian, 'The gods
12 have come down to us in human form.' And they called
Barnabas Jupiter, and Paul they called Mercury, because
13 he was the spokesman. And the priest of Jupiter, whose
temple was just outside the city, brought oxen and garlands to the gates, and he and all the people were about
to offer sacrifice.

14 But when the apostles Barnabas and Paul heard of it,
they tore their clothes and rushed into the crowd shouting,
15 'Men, what is this that you are doing? We are only
human beings, no less mortal than you. The good news
we bring tells you to turn from these follies to the living
God, who made heaven and earth and sea and everything
16 in them. In past ages he allowed all nations to go their
17 own way; and yet he has not left you without some clue
to his nature, in the kindness he shows: he sends you rain
from heaven and crops in their seasons, and gives you
food and good cheer in plenty.'

18 With these words they barely managed to prevent the
crowd from offering sacrifice to them.

19 Then Jews from Antioch and Iconium came on the scene
and won over the crowds. They stoned Paul, and dragged
20 him out of the city, thinking him dead. The converts
formed a ring round him, and he got to his feet and went
into the city. Next day he left with Barnabas for Derbe.

After bringing the good news to that town, where they 21
gained many converts, they returned to Lystra, then to
Iconium, and then to Antioch, heartening the converts 22
and encouraging them to be true to their religion. They
warned them that to enter the kingdom of God we must
pass through many hardships. They also appointed elders 23
for them in each congregation, and with prayer and
fasting committed them to the Lord in whom they had
put their faith.

Then they passed through Pisidia and came into Pam- 24
phylia. When they had given the message at Perga, they 25
went down to Attalia, and from there set sail for Antioch, 26
where they had originally been commended to the grace
of God for the task which they had now completed. When 27
they arrived and had called the congregation together,
they reported all that God had helped them to do, and
how he had thrown open the gates of faith to the Gentiles.
And they stayed for some time with the disciples there. 28

* A new phase in the preaching of the Way is imminent. So
far the normal practice of the missionaries had been to begin
their work in the synagogues amongst Jews and 'God-fearers',
and this method was to continue. The good news then spread
to the Gentiles who, through genuine inquiry or mere
curiosity, showed themselves interested. Before long this must
involve contact, even conflict, with heathen religion. Events
at Lystra showed what Paul's policy was likely to be, and may
be compared with what took place in Athens (17: 16–34) and
Ephesus (19: 23–41).

1. *similarly*: i.e. in the same way as at Antioch (to Jews and
'God-fearers' in the synagogues) rather than 'together' as in
the R.V. and R.S.V. and the N.E.B. footnote.

2–3. These verses do not read smoothly. Verse 2 suggests

that the Jews began to create trouble almost at once, whereas verse 3 speaks of Paul and Barnabas at work in Iconium for some time before 'a move was made by Gentiles and Jews together, with the connivance of the city authorities, to maltreat them' (verse 5).

3. The signs of the Spirit are apparent—bold and open speech *in reliance on the Lord*, confirmed by *signs and miracles to be worked at their hands* (cf. the very similar work of Peter and the Twelve in Jerusalem, 5: 12–16).

4. The town is thereby divided between the supporters of the Jews and the supporters of *the apostles*—the word is used by Luke to mean 'missionaries', i.e. those sent by the church (cf. the appointment by the commissioning committee in Antioch, 13: 3).

5. *move*: 'attempt' (R.S.V.), 'onset' (R.V.) are not quite so clear.

with the connivance of the city authorities: literally, 'with their rulers'. The N.E.B. clearly assumes that the opposition to the apostles had the support, at least passively, of the *city authorities*, and not only that of the rulers of the synagogue.

to maltreat them and stone them: gives the impression of mob-violence, as when Stephen was killed (7: 58).

6–7. *Lystra*: 23 miles south-west of Iconium, a Roman colony in Lycaonia.

Derbe: 56 miles south-east of Lystra. Paul and Barnabas did not confine their work to these cities but *spread the good news* to the surrounding villages. Timothy may well have been converted during this visit (16: 1–2).

8–18. The healing at Lystra is a close parallel to that at the Beautiful Gate in Jerusalem (3: 1–10). Crippled from birth, the men in both instances have faith to be healed, as Peter and Paul realized, when they *looked* them *in the face* (verse 9; 'Peter fixed his eyes on him', 3: 4). It was the sign of God's presence in their midst whereby his Spirit acted through his disciples.

11–13. The result of the sign was that the crowd took Paul and Barnabas for gods walking the earth. The setting of the local legend is given by Ovid (*Metamorphoses* VIII. 626 ff.). Zeus (Jupiter) and Hermes (Mercury), perhaps Greek names given to local gods (cf. 'Artemis' or 'Diana' at Ephesus, 19: 24), visited Philemon and Baucis in Phrygia. Inscriptions of later date to Zeus and Hermes have been found in the neighbourhood. The crowd, which would probably have spoken Greek, reverted to its own local dialect for its worship. Perhaps they regarded Barnabas as the superior, Jupiter, because of his silent presence and Paul as his *spokesman*, Mercury (verse 12), uttering the divine oracles. The accuracy of Luke's report of the episode is confirmed by this reversal of order in the apostles' names, since from the beginning of the mission to Asia Minor when Paul became the leader (13: 13), his name has been given first; the order is in the same way reversed at Jerusalem (15: 12) where Barnabas takes his place as the senior.

13. The sign would seem to have taken place at the city gates (perhaps the cripple was begging there; cf. at the Beautiful Gate in Jerusalem, 3: 2) and the oxen with garlands of wool round their necks would be sacrificed there.

14-17. Paul and Barnabas seized the opportunity afforded them. This was a situation they could use to the glory of God (cf. Peter and the apostles after the tragedy of Ananias and Sapphira, 5: 11-16). *They tore their clothes*, not at the blasphemy (cf. the High Priest at Jesus' trial, Mark 14: 63), but to draw attention to their distress as they *rushed into the crowd shouting*. There is nothing specifically Christian in what they said. The challenge is to turn from the *follies* of idolatry to the worship of *the living God*, the creator. When Paul spoke to a more intellectual pagan audience in Athens (17: 22-31), he began in much the same way but explained *the good news* (14: 15) as the assurance God had given by raising the 'man of his choosing' from the dead (17: 31). God's revelation through nature has been available to all men 'ever since the world began' (see Paul's argument in Rom. 1: 18-23), but if they refused to understand *he allowed all nations to go their own way*.

As Paul said to the Romans, 'knowing God, they have refused to honour him as God, or to render him thanks' (Rom. 1: 21).

18. It was an uncertain victory, as this and the next verse show, but seeds had been sown and the apostles returned to Lystra on the way back (verse 21). Later, when Timothy joined Paul on his next visit, there must have been a considerable company of Christians in the city (16: 1–3).

19–20. The lightning change in the attitude of the crowd at Lystra, when *Jews from Antioch and Iconium* caught up with Paul and Barnabas, is reminiscent of that similar change between Palm Sunday (Luke 19: 37–8) and Good Friday (Luke 23: 18–21) in the attitude of the Jerusalem crowd towards Jesus.

Paul refers to this stoning in 2 Cor. 11: 25. He must have been severely stunned to be thought dead. Presumably the authorities were prepared to hand over his body to his friends for burial (cf. Jesus, Luke 23: 50–3). His recovery and departure next day for Derbe say much for his stamina and will-power.

21–3. The mission to Derbe seems to have been entirely successful. Perhaps the town was too far away for the trouble-makers to follow. The return journey via Lystra, Iconium and Antioch was courageous (they could have gone direct to Syria) but essential for the well-being of the converts. In the midst of a hostile world, they would need *heartening...and encouraging* and none could do that better than Paul and Barnabas. Furthermore, the departure of the apostles had been too hasty for a proper organization to be set up in each town. This could also now be remedied. As there seems to be no outward hostility to the apostles on the return journey, they possibly confined themselves to work amongst the converts.

22. *their religion*: literally, 'the Faith' as in 13: 8. The N.E.B. is probably right in interpreting it as *their religion*, i.e. Christianity.

Persecution was to come to them, as it came to Jesus and as he promised it would come to his disciples (John 15: 20,

'As they persecuted me, they will persecute you'). The reward will be 'the kingship which my Father vested in me' (Luke 22: 29).

23. Just as Paul and Barnabas had been appointed for this mission by the committee in Antioch with prayer and fasting (13: 3), so now they *appointed elders for them in each congregation* in the same way.

elders: the organization resembles that of the synagogue and possibly follows the pattern of the Jerusalem church (11: 30). The word presbyters (elders) probably meant the senior members of the local church at this stage. They formed its governing body and were responsible for its worship, charity and discipline.

the Lord in whom they had put their faith: i.e. Jesus, in whom they now believed.

24–5. The return journey led through the districts of Pisidia and Pamphylia, where they paused to spread the good news in Perga.

26–8. They sailed direct from Attalia to Syria without revisiting Cyprus, and reported back to those who had commissioned them for the journey. Behind all their work had been the direction of God's Holy Spirit and *he had thrown open the gates of faith to the Gentiles*. The deed had been done and all in Antioch believed it was God, through his disciples, who had done it. Would the Jerusalem church think the same? For the present, however, Paul and Barnabas remained in the fellowship of the church in Antioch. ✳

THE GREAT DECISION

Now certain persons who had come down from Judaea **15** began to teach the brotherhood that those who were not circumcised in accordance with Mosaic practice could not be saved. That brought them into fierce dissension **2** and controversy with Paul and Barnabas. And so it was arranged that these two and some others from Antioch should go up to Jerusalem to see the apostles and elders about this question.

3   They were sent on their way by the congregation, and travelled through Phoenicia and Samaria, telling the full story of the conversion of the Gentiles. The news caused great rejoicing among all the Christians there.

4   When they reached Jerusalem they were welcomed by the church and the apostles and elders, and reported all
5 that God had helped them to do. Then some of the Pharisaic party who had become believers came forward and said, 'They must be circumcised and told to keep the Law of Moses.'

6   The apostles and elders held a meeting to look into this
7 matter; and, after a long debate, Peter rose and addressed them. 'My friends,' he said, 'in the early days, as you yourselves know, God made his choice among you and ordained that from my lips the Gentiles should hear and
8 believe the message of the Gospel. And God, who can read men's minds, showed his approval of them by giving
9 the Holy Spirit to them, as he did to us. He made no difference between them and us; for he purified their
10 hearts by faith. Then why do you now provoke God by laying on the shoulders of these converts a yoke which
11 neither we nor our fathers were able to bear? No, we believe that it is by the grace of the Lord Jesus that we are saved, and so are they.'

12   At that the whole company fell silent and listened to Barnabas and Paul as they told of all the signs and miracles that God had worked among the Gentiles through them.

13   When they had finished speaking, James summed up:

120

'My friends,' he said, 'listen to me. Simeon has told how 14
it first happened that God took notice of the Gentiles, to
choose from among them a people to bear his name; and 15
this agrees with the words of the prophets, as Scripture
has it:

"Thereafter I will return and rebuild the fallen house of 16
    David;
Even from its ruins I will rebuild it, and set it up again,
That they may seek the Lord—all the rest of mankind, 17
And the Gentiles, whom I have claimed for my own.
Thus says the Lord, whose work it is,
Made known long ago." 18

'My judgement therefore is that we should impose no 19
irksome restrictions on those of the Gentiles who are
turning to God, but instruct them by letter to abstain from 20
things polluted by contact with idols, from fornication,
from anything that has been strangled, and from blood.
Moses, after all, has never lacked spokesmen in every town 21
for generations past; he is read in the synagogues Sabbath
by Sabbath.'

Then the apostles and elders, with the agreement of the 22
whole church, resolved to choose representatives and send
them to Antioch with Paul and Barnabas. They chose two
leading men in the community, Judas Barsabbas and Silas,
and gave them this letter to deliver: 23

'We, the apostles and elders, send greetings as brothers
to our brothers of gentile origin in Antioch, Syria, and
Cilicia. Forasmuch as we have heard that some of our 24
number, without any instructions from us, have disturbed
you with their talk and unsettled your minds, we have 25

resolved unanimously to send to you our chosen repre-
26 sentatives with our well-beloved Barnabas and Paul, who
have devoted themselves to the cause of our Lord Jesus
27 Christ. We are therefore sending Judas and Silas, who
28 will themselves confirm this by word of mouth. It is the
decision of the Holy Spirit, and our decision, to lay no
29 further burden upon you beyond these essentials: you are
to abstain from meat that has been offered to idols, from
blood, from anything that has been strangled, and from
fornication. If you keep yourselves free from these things
you will be doing right. Farewell.'

30 So they were sent off on their journey and travelled
down to Antioch, where they called the congregation
31 together, and delivered the letter. When it was read, they
32 all rejoiced at the encouragement it brought. Judas and
Silas, who were prophets themselves, said much to en-
33 courage and strengthen the members, and, after spending
some time there, were dismissed with the good wishes of
35 the brethren, to return to those who had sent them. But
Paul and Barnabas stayed on at Antioch, and there, along
with many others. they taught and preached the word of
the Lord.

* A great deal of speculation has for a long time surrounded
this chapter. There is no doubt that Luke regarded the decisions of the meeting as of great importance for the expansion
of the church. It is less clear that Paul so regarded them. He
never refers to them in his letters, even when he is discussing
food problems in Rom. 14 and 1 Cor. 8 and 10. He may have
specifically avoided doing so as his ideas may have been more
liberal. 'You may eat anything sold in the meat-market
without raising questions of conscience; for the earth is the
Lord's and everything in it' (1 Cor. 10: 25–6). The meeting

at Jerusalem gave a decision based on Jewish Law and had instructed Gentiles by letter *to abstain from meat that has been offered to idols, from blood, from anything that has been strangled* (verse 29). In his letters Paul preferred to argue out the matter, appealing to the conscience of those he addressed.

The approbation that had been given in Jerusalem after Peter's explanation of what he had done at Cornelius' house in Caesarea was clearly *not* unanimous, or if it had been, some had now had second thoughts. 'When they heard this their doubts were silenced' (11: 18) is more of hope than fact. It may well be that those *who had come down from Judaea* and *began to teach the brotherhood that those who were not circumcised in accordance with Mosaic practice could not be saved* (verse 1) were the same as those who had earlier challenged Peter with 'You have been visiting men who are uncircumcised and sitting at table with them!' (11: 3). In fact these Judaizers, changing from one side to the other, were liable to wreck the boat. It is no wonder that it brought them into *fierce dissension and controversy with Paul and Barnabas* when they arrived in Antioch. One gains the impression that the two missionaries, whose work among the Gentiles in Asia Minor had met with such success and had been so approved in Antioch, went up to Jerusalem with some other companions to have the business settled once and for all in consultation with *the apostles and elders.*

The meeting was certainly impressive. Paul and Barnabas arrived flushed with a sort of triumphal progress *through Phoenicia and Samaria, telling the full story of the conversion of the Gentiles* amidst great rejoicings. They were welcomed by the Christian community in Jerusalem and made their report. Then *some of the Pharisaic party who had become believers came forward and said, ' They* (the converted Gentiles) *must be circumcised and told to keep the Law of Moses'* (verse 5).

It seems strange that when the meeting was called Peter only made his vital contribution *after a long debate*, and then he speaks of his experiences at Joppa and Caesarea (as one supposes him to mean) as *in the early days*. Had Peter's influence waned in the Jerusalem church since he 'went off elsewhere' (12: 17) or had he been in semi-retirement after his imprisonment?

It would have seemed more likely for Barnabas and Paul (the reversion to the old order of seniority would be natural in Jerusalem) to have *told of all the signs and miracles that God had worked among the Gentiles through them* early in the debate, but perhaps the assembly was too argumentative to listen to a straight statement of the facts until Peter had spoken (cf. *the whole company fell silent*, verse 12). James' summing up (verses 13-21) with no more discussion seems a hurried conclusion to the debate. The impression is left that 'the chairman' ended the meeting before any further opposition arose. Was the whole church in agreement with the apostles and elders or were the Judaizers merely silenced and licking their wounds? They had carried the day only to the extent that Gentiles must keep the food laws and abstain from fornication (see note below on verse 20); but they had not persuaded their colleagues that converted Gentiles must be circumcised.

If there were a sense of frustration on the part of some, it would account for the astonishing statement in Gal. 2: 11-13 that when Peter was in Antioch he took his meals with gentile Christians 'until certain persons came from James'. Then 'he drew back and began to hold aloof, because he was afraid of the advocates of circumcision. The other Jewish Christians showed the same lack of principle; even Barnabas was carried away and played false like the rest'. If, as some scholars believe, Galatians was written by Paul to encourage his converts as soon as he returned to Antioch but after the Judaizers had come from Judaea (15: 1), then this might account for the behaviour of Peter and Barnabas and the fact that there is no reference to the Jerusalem meeting in the letter. On the other hand, if Barnabas had been involved in this way, he would seem an odd choice as a delegate from the church at Antioch, and Peter's speech in Jerusalem must have resulted in part from Paul's rebuke (Gal. 2: 11).

Any attempt to fit together Paul's visits to Jerusalem as narrated in Acts with those in Galatians is fraught with difficulties. Acts has three visits—after the conversion (9: 26–30), in response to the famine appeal (11: 27–30; 12: 25), and the visit to the council (15: 2 ff.); Galatians has two—three years after the conversion (1: 18–20) and fourteen years later with Barnabas and Titus (2: 1–5). The first in each case probably correspond but the visit accompanied by Titus could have been in response to Agabus' prediction (i.e. 'it had been revealed by God that I should do so', Gal. 2: 2), or may correspond with the council visit, where there were certainly Judaizers who wanted 'to bring us into bondage' (Gal. 2: 4). This latter is, however, 'a private interview with the men of repute' (Gal. 2: 2) and the council meeting is hardly that.

Perhaps it is a waste of time to try to harmonize Acts and Galatians. We do not know how often Paul visited Jerusalem, nor with whom. We do know his visits often involved strain (cf. 9: 26, 29–30; Gal. 2: 5). It is impossible to believe that all went smoothly at the council. It was *a long debate* (15: 7). Paul was a turbulent missionary and enjoyed being so. The council decision was a personal victory for him and, as such, a vindication of his liberal action in Asia Minor and of his point of view. Contact with the officials at Jerusalem was a difficult business, to be avoided whenever possible! The importance with which Paul regarded the letter issued by the Jerusalem church may be an indication of his relationship with its members. Apart from the fact that he and Silas on the next journey through Asia Minor 'handed on the decisions taken by the apostles and elders in Jerusalem and enjoined their observance' (16: 4), we hear no more of them in Acts, except the reference in 21: 25, and not at all in the Letters, though the church observed them for some time to come.

It is of course true that Luke described the debate in stylized form and thus we have no clue to the real order of events. He wishes it to be understood that the meeting eventually came to one mind, that its decision was prepared for by previous events, and that no disagreement with the decision could be permitted afterwards. Nevertheless Luke was well aware that many Jewish Christians did not approve of the admission of uncircumcised Gentiles into the church, and lest they should feel that the decision might lead to the refusal of circumcision by Jewish Christians, he stresses Paul's actions in accordance with the Law at Lystra (16: 3), at Cenchreae (18: 18) and in Jerusalem (21: 23-6)

2. The *dissension* was *fierce*. Perhaps the Christians in Antioch had not expected such interference from Jerusalem, in view of the happy agreement after the conversion of Cornelius (11: 18).

5. *the Pharisaic party* amongst the Jewish Christians in Jerusalem would be the conservative group and so moved by the most serious considerations of the meaning of the Law.

7. *the Gospel*: in Acts, the word, *euangelion* or 'good news', occurs only here and in Paul's speech to the elders of Ephesus at Miletus (20: 24). In both speeches there is a sense of farewell, with the conviction that both apostles have carried out their appointed task of bearing their 'testimony to the gospel of God's grace' (20: 24).

10-11. Instead of the Law being a joy to those under it, it had been turned into 'intolerable burdens', as Jesus said (Luke 11: 46), for the Jews themselves. For Gentiles it would be impossible and unnecessary to bear it, for, said Peter: *we believe that it is by the grace of the Lord Jesus that we are saved, and so are they*.

12. Peter's speech at last opens the door for Paul and Barnabas to report on the way in which the Holy Spirit had shown his directing presence among the Gentiles.

13-21. James is clearly leader of the Jerusalem church and, as such, is mentioned before Peter and John in Gal. 2: 9. He refers to Peter by the Semitic form of his name, Simeon (see 2 Pet. 1: 1)—identification with anyone else of the name, e.g. Simeon Niger (13: 1), seems entirely out of place—perhaps as a sop to the Pharisaic party, but he quotes from the Greek

(Septuagint) Bible from Amos 9: 11–12. This version is more to the point than the Hebrew 'that they' (Israel) 'may possess the remnant of Edom, and all the nations which are called by my name'. In the Hebrew text the same letters can be read as Edom and Adam (i.e. mankind), which may well account for the variation.

15. *the words of the prophets*: that part of the Old Testament scriptures known as the Prophets, i.e. the historical books (Joshua to Kings) and the prophetic books.

16–17. *fallen house*: literally, 'tent' or 'tabernacle'. The N.E.B. correctly implies David's kingdom, rebuilt for *all the rest of mankind, And the Gentiles, whom I have claimed for my own*.

18. *Made known long ago*: some suggest that this is an addition to the quotation from Amos from Isa. 45: 21, but it would seem much more probable that the Amos text here—which in its last verses is stylistically very much like Second Isaiah (i.e. chapters 40–55)—has a variant introducing a longer ending to the passage.

19. *no irksome restrictions*: this is the only reference to the main points at issue—circumcision and the Mosaic Law—but it comes strongly from James.

20. There is a textual problem here. As it stands, the prohibitions are four: *to abstain from things polluted by contact with idols*, i.e. from eating meat offered in idol temples and then sold in the shops whereby the purchaser partook in idol worship; *from fornication*, i.e. mixed marriages with pagans, marriages within prohibited degrees or perhaps lax heathen relationships; *from anything that has been strangled, and from blood*, i.e. any meat containing blood 'for the life of the flesh is in the blood: and I have given it to you upon the altar to make atonement for your souls' (Lev. 17: 11). Some manuscripts omit the second prohibition and some the third but add at the end, 'and to refrain from doing to others what they would not like done to themselves'. This turns a food regulation into a moral command and makes *blood* mean 'murder'. This would seem a later development. The emphasis here is on the

relationship between Jewish and gentile members of the church and its expression most prominently in the Jewish marriage and food laws. The same variants occur in the letter (verse 29).

21. Various interpretations have been given for this verse, e.g. that the Gentiles ought to be aware of the requirements of the Law, for it is read weekly in synagogues all over the world; or that *Jewish* Christians must observe the whole Law. Perhaps it means that the abrogation of the Law for Gentiles will not affect Moses. He is capable of looking after himself. There are plenty of orthodox Jews (and Jewish Christians) who will hear him *Sabbath by Sabbath*.

It has been suggested that Luke has combined the work of two committees of the Jerusalem church in this report of the council's decision—namely, one on circumcision and the Law and another on food regulations—thus allowing for the fact that there is no direct reference to the purpose of the visit of Paul and Barnabas in either the decision or the letter. James, however, may have been wise enough, after a heated meeting, to have skilfully hidden the greater point behind the lesser and thereby got it through. (See above, pp. 122–4.)

22. This verse implies that the decision was unanimous, which gives it added weight.

Judas Barsabbas and Silas were prominent members of the Jerusalem church and prophets (verse 32). Judas has the same additional name as Joseph in 1: 23. Silas is almost certainly the Silvanus of Paul's letters (2 Cor. 1: 19; and in the address of both letters to the Thessalonians). He was Paul's companion on his next expedition (15: 40) and may well be the Silvanus of 1 Pet. 5: 12.

23–9. The letter repeats James' judgement. It is sent from *the apostles and elders* of the Jerusalem church to the gentile Christians *in Antioch, Syria and Cilicia* (not the district of Paul's recent activities in Galatia, though he handed on the decisions there on his next visit, 16: 4).

24–6. They disavowed responsibility for their colleagues' visit to Antioch (15: 1) *without any instructions from us*, and spoke affectionately of Barnabas and Paul, *who have devoted themselves to the cause of our Lord Jesus Christ.*

cause: literally, 'name', reflecting the idea of their possession by Jesus.

27. The letter is to be confirmed by word of mouth.

28. Once again the Holy Spirit is at work confirming the decision of the church (cf. Peter's reply to the High Priest, 'we are witnesses to all this, and so is the Holy Spirit', 5: 32).

30–5. The joy of the church at Antioch on the receipt of the letter was increased by the exhortation of Judas and Silas, *who were prophets themselves* (cf. Agabus and his associates 11: 27–8).

(34) 'But Silas decided to remain there' is added in some manuscripts to explain the fact that he accompanied Paul on the next expedition (verse 40).

35. Peace descends on the church at Antioch once again, with Paul and Barnabas at work *with many others* (cf. 13: 1; 14: 28). *

Paul Leads the Advance

'COME ACROSS TO MACEDONIA AND HELP US' (16: 9)

AFTER A WHILE Paul said to Barnabas, 'Ought we not 36 to go back now to see how our brothers are faring in the various towns where we proclaimed the word of the Lord?' Barnabas wanted to take John Mark with 37 them; but Paul judged that the man who had deserted 38 them in Pamphylia and had not gone on to share in their work was not the man to take with them now. The dis- 39 pute was so sharp that they parted company. Barnabas took Mark with him and sailed for Cyprus, while Paul 40

Through Asia Minor to Troas

chose Silas. He started on his journey, commended by
41 the brothers to the grace of the Lord, and travelled
through Syria and Cilicia bringing new strength to the
congregations.

16　He went on to Derbe and to Lystra, and there he found
a disciple named Timothy, the son of a Jewish Christian
2 mother and a Greek father. He was well spoken of by the
3 Christians at Lystra and Iconium, and Paul wanted to have
him in his company when he left the place. So he took
him and circumcised him, out of consideration for the
Jews who lived in those parts; for they all knew that his
4 father was a Greek. As they made their way from town
to town they handed on the decisions taken by the apostles

and elders in Jerusalem and enjoined their observance.
And so, day by day, the congregations grew stronger in 5
faith and increased in numbers.

They travelled through the Phrygian and Galatian re- 6
gion, because they were prevented by the Holy Spirit from
delivering the message in the province of Asia; and when 7
they approached the Mysian border they tried to enter
Bithynia; but the Spirit of Jesus would not allow them,
so they skirted Mysia and reached the coast at Troas. 8
During the night a vision came to Paul: a Macedonian 9
stood there appealing to him and saying, 'Come across
to Macedonia and help us.' After he had seen this vision 10
we at once set about getting a passage to Macedonia, concluding that God had called us to bring them the good
news.

∗ This time Paul's progress through Asia Minor is only a
prelude to the European mission which begins in 16: 11.
A wider horizon is opening up for the Christian church and
Paul is eager to move forward into new territory as quickly
as possible.

15: 36–41. Luke is here covering up as briefly as possible
what was obviously an unpleasant episode between Paul and
Barnabas. *The dispute was so sharp that they parted company*
(verse 39). Nothing was said in 13: 13 of John's reasons for
leaving Paul's party in Pamphylia on the first visit and no
explanation is given here for Paul's annoyance about it. One
is left to wonder whether Luke's silence indicates a feeling on
his part that Paul was unreasonable. If so, it throws an
interesting sidelight on the characters of the men concerned.

36. Paul takes his apostleship seriously in the sense of an
overseer of the churches founded by himself and Barnabas.

39. The dispute resulted in a division of labour: Barnabas
and Mark went to the churches in Cyprus, Paul and Silas to

those on the mainland. It seems sad that Paul's sponsor, when he was introduced to the apostles in Jerusalem (9: 27), should disappear so abruptly from the stage at this point. Dramatic dismissals of this sort are very much in Luke's style. Exeunt Barnabas and Mark. Enter Silas and Timothy. The breach was not permanent, as is shown in 1 Cor. 9: 6 where Paul links Barnabas with himself in the work of an apostle. Mark is mentioned as a worker with Paul in Col. 4: 10, Philem. 24 and 2 Tim. 4: 11.

40. Silas had been brought from Jerusalem, unless verse 34 is accepted as explanation of his presence still in Antioch. He continued in the party at least as far as Corinth and his name (Silvanus) is associated with those of Paul and Timothy in the address at the beginning of the Letters to the Thessalonians.

41. Paul's work in Syria and Cilicia is referred to in Gal. 1: 21.

16: 1–5. Timothy joins the expedition. Timothy's entry into the story is as dramatic as Mark's exit and he replaces him as Paul's companion; his name appears in the address of many of Paul's letters. The selection of Timothy is especially appropriate. He had a foot in both camps—a Jew on his mother's side and a Gentile on his father's—and thus Paul saw fit to have him circumcised before he joined the official mission. The circumcision of Timothy shows no inconsistency in Paul, who never spoke or acted as if he believed that the Law ceased to be binding for a Jew. Timothy was known to have a Jewish mother (which since the return from the Baby-lonian exile had become the criterion, and still is, whether a man was a Jew or not) but a gentile father, so might be known to have been neglected as far as circumcision is concerned. The circumcision of Timothy therefore is not at all contrary to the Jerusalem decrees, which failed to enjoin circumcision for Gentiles (cf. the comment on the 'vow' in 21: 20–4). Timothy's background is interesting. Brought up a Gentile, *he was well spoken of by the Christians at Lystra and Iconium.* Perhaps Timothy, his mother Eunice, and his grandmother Lois

(2 Tim. 1: 5), had been converted on Paul's earlier visit. Whatever Timothy's family relationships at this time may have been, they were a good background for a Jewish-gentile mission.

4. Paul acts very correctly as a representative of the Jerusalem church by handing on the decisions of the apostles and elders and enjoining their observance.

6–10. To the coast. It may be that a considerable amount of missionary activity is telescoped into these verses, but the general impression is that, contrary to their own inclinations, the missionaries were inspired by the Holy Spirit (whom Luke purposefully calls *the Spirit of Jesus* (verse 7), thereby reinforcing the idea that Jesus was accompanying the mission through the Spirit) to avoid the tempting fields of the province of Asia, Bithynia and Mysia and reach the coast as soon as possible.

Too much may well have been read into the phrase *Phrygian and Galatian region* or 'Phrygia and the Galatian region' (N.E.B. footnote). If it means the province of Galatia or the district inhabited by the Galatians then it might imply a detour to the north, and the letter to the Galatians may have been written to the people of this area; but the likelihood seems to be that Paul and his companions kept south, taking his earlier route in the reverse direction, originally aiming for Ephesus.

8. *Troas*: the seaport on the north-west coast of Asia Minor.

9–10. The direction of the Holy Spirit has been emphasized all through this journey so far and now Paul feels that, through his vision of the man of Macedonia, *God had called us to bring them the good news*. The fact that the first 'we-section' begins here led to the intriguing suggestion that Luke himself was the Macedonian (see above, p. 3), but there is no reason to suppose that the author was not already one of the party. It is also a possible conjecture that Luke joined Paul at Troas because of the latter's need of a doctor there either on this occasion or later (20: 1–2). *

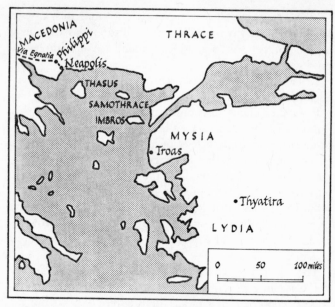

The arrival in Europe

EUROPE AT LAST

11 So we sailed from Troas and made a straight run to
12 Samothrace, the next day to Neapolis, and from there to
Philippi, a city of the first rank in that district of Macedonia, and a Roman colony. Here we stayed for some
13 days, and on the Sabbath day we went outside the city
gate by the river-side, where we thought there would be
a place of prayer, and sat down and talked to the women
14 who had gathered there. One of them named Lydia,
a dealer in purple fabric from the city of Thyatira, who
was a worshipper of God, was listening, and the Lord
15 opened her heart to respond to what Paul said. She was
baptized, and her household with her, and then she said

to us, 'If you have judged me to be a believer in the Lord,
I beg you to come and stay in my house.' And she insisted
on our going.

✱ 11. *Samothrace*: a mountainous island in the Aegean, a useful
half-way port of call on the voyage from Asia to Europe. It
must have been a favourable journey as it only took two days.
The return in 20: 6 took five.

Neapolis: the port of Philippi and the end of the east–west
route across Greece, the Via Egnatia, which joined Rome and
Asia.

12. *Philippi*: made a colony by Augustus, and an important
town. *A city of the first rank* does not mean the capital of
Macedonia, which was Thessalonica, nor of the local district,
which was Amphipolis. It was an important, rapidly growing
city in its own right.

13. *a place of prayer*: the Jewish community must have been
small not to have any regular synagogue. Some manuscripts
read 'where there was a recognized place of prayer' for *where
we thought there would be a place of prayer*.

14. *Lydia*: Thyatira was the centre of the purple-dye
industry in the district of Lydia in the province of Asia; thus
her name may be a nickname or refer to her home district.
She was a 'God-fearer', i.e. she *was a worshipper of God*.

15. Lydia's house becomes the centre of the church in
Philippi. ✱

THE SLAVE-GIRL—AND THE MAGISTRATES

Once, when we were on our way to the place of prayer, 16
we met a slave-girl who was possessed by an oracular
spirit and brought large profits to her owners by telling
fortunes. She followed Paul and the rest of us, shouting, 17
'These men are servants of the Supreme God, and are
declaring to you a way of salvation.' She did this day 18

after day, until Paul could bear it no longer. Rounding on the spirit he said, 'I command you in the name of Jesus Christ to come out of her', and it went out there and then.

19 When the girl's owners saw that their hope of gain had gone, they seized Paul and Silas and dragged them to the
20 city authorities in the main square; and bringing them before the magistrates, they said, 'These men are causing
21 a disturbance in our city; they are Jews; they are advocating customs which it is illegal for us Romans to adopt
22 and follow.' The mob joined in the attack; and the magistrates tore off the prisoners' clothes and ordered them to
23 be flogged. After giving them a severe beating they flung them into prison and ordered the jailer to keep them under
24 close guard. In view of these orders, he put them in the inner prison and secured their feet in the stocks.

25 About midnight Paul and Silas, at their prayers, were singing praises to God, and the other prisoners were
26 listening, when suddenly there was such a violent earthquake that the foundations of the jail were shaken; all the doors burst open and all the prisoners found their fetters
27 unfastened. The jailer woke up to see the prison doors wide open, and assuming that the prisoners had escaped,
28 drew his sword intending to kill himself. But Paul
29 shouted, 'Do yourself no harm; we are all here.' The jailer called for lights, rushed in and threw himself down
30 before Paul and Silas, trembling with fear. He then escorted them out and said, 'Masters, what must I do to
31 be saved?' They said, 'Put your trust in the Lord Jesus,
32 and you will be saved, you and your household.' Then they spoke the word of the Lord to him and to everyone
33 in his house. At that late hour of the night he took them

and washed their wounds; and immediately afterwards
he and his whole family were baptized. He brought them 34
into his house, set out a meal, and rejoiced with his whole
household in his new-found faith in God.

When daylight came the magistrates sent their officers 35
with instructions to release the men. The jailer reported 36
the message to Paul: 'The magistrates have sent word
that you are to be released. So now you may go free, and
blessings on your journey.' But Paul said to the officers: 37
'They gave us a public flogging, though we are Roman
citizens and have not been found guilty; they threw us
into prison, and are they now to smuggle us out privately?
No indeed! Let them come in person and escort us out.'
The officers reported his words. The magistrates were 38
alarmed to hear that they were Roman citizens, and came 39
and apologized to them. Then they escorted them out
and requested them to go away from the city. On leaving 40
the prison, they went to Lydia's house, where they met
their fellow-Christians, and spoke words of encouragement to them; then they departed.

✻ Once again Luke exhibits in this chapter his powers of
making the reader feel at home. Without describing Philippi
he deftly inserts a piece or two of local colour—the place of
prayer outside the gate, the river, Lydia's house, the main
square, the prison—and then peoples the scene with a cross-
section of the community—the pious Jewesses; Lydia, the
woman of business; the slave-girl; those who exploited her;
the magistrates; the mob; the prisoners; the jailer and, among
them all, Paul and Silas.

16. The *slave-girl* was used by her owners to make money.
an oracular spirit: literally, 'a python', the name of the dragon
slain by Apollo at Delphi. Thereafter Apollo was held to be

137

embodied in a python, and so a python spirit was an Apollo spirit, i.e. a spirit by which the god spoke to the person who had it, and enabled her to pronounce oracles. This encounter resembles that of Philip with Simon (8: 9–13) and of Paul and Barnabas with Bar-Jesus (13: 6–12).

17. *the Supreme God*: the same title is used by the Gadarene demoniac who may also have been a pagan (Luke 8: 28).

18. *in the name of Jesus Christ*: the exorcism took this form, as had the healing of the cripple at the Beautiful Gate (3: 6).

19–23. The owners of the slave-girl were naturally furious, and used anti-Jewish feeling to influence the magistrates. Although Judaism was protected by Roman law, proselytizing was illegal. The missionary work of Paul and Silas could easily be included under this head.

19. *city authorities*: *archontes*, a general term for the city fathers.

20. *magistrates*: *strategoi* or *praetors*, as the *duoviri* (the title given to provincial magistrates) were called, were the chief of police in the Roman colony and entitled to *lictors* or *officers* (verse 35) to carry out their orders.

24. The imprisonment resembles closely Peter's in 12: 1–10. In both, emphasis is placed on the security of the precautions taken, probably to stress the miraculous nature of the deliverance.

25–6. Paul and Silas use their predicament to witness by prayers and hymns to their faith in God, and the earthquake is a confirmation of it.

27. The jailer's intended suicide was obviously to forestall the execution he would suffer if the prisoners escaped, as happened after Peter's release (12: 19).

31. *you and your household*: as with Lydia (verse 15), so with the jailer, their households were baptized with them. The household was regarded as the unit. 'Crispus...with all his household' became believers 'in the Lord' at Corinth (18: 8). The company at Cornelius' house similarly received a mass baptism (10: 48).

34. The meal in the jailer's house is a further touch of local colour.

35–40. The apology. The law forbade the scourging of Roman citizens, even if condemned. Paul and Silas had *not* even *been found guilty*. Luke clearly intends his readers to note that Roman law befriended Christians. Paul's protest is magnificently proclaimed—*are they now to smuggle us out privately? No indeed! Let them come in person and escort us out.*

40. *On leaving the prison, they went to Lydia's house* as Peter did to Mary's (12: 12). The stories seem consciously parallel. Paul is following the same pattern in a gentile environment as Peter did in a Jewish. The work of the two apostles corresponds.

Now the European mission was fairly launched in 'a city of the first rank in that district of Macedonia, and a Roman colony' (16: 12). It was a cosmopolitan city—Jews, Asiatics, Greeks and Romans meeting together. Paul and Silas had made contact with them all and, through suffering, came out triumphant. It was a period for the renewal of confidence and determination for the unknown tasks ahead. ✳

INTO THE HEART OF GREECE

PART I—TO ATHENS: (*a*) ON THE WAY

They now travelled by way of Amphipolis and Apollonia **17** and came to Thessalonica, where there was a Jewish synagogue. Following his usual practice Paul went to 2 their meetings; and for the next three Sabbaths he argued with them, quoting texts of Scripture which he expounded 3 and applied to show that the Messiah had to suffer and rise from the dead. 'And this Jesus,' he said, 'whom I am proclaiming to you, is the Messiah.' Some of them were 4 convinced and joined Paul and Silas; so did a great number of godfearing Greeks and a good many influential women.

But the Jews in their jealousy recruited some low fellows 5

Paul in Macedonia and Achaia

from the dregs of the populace, roused the rabble, and had the city in an uproar. They mobbed Jason's house, with the intention of bringing Paul and Silas before the
6 town assembly. Failing to find them, they dragged Jason himself and some members of the congregation before the

magistrates, shouting, 'The men who have made trouble all
over the world have now come here; and Jason has har- 7
boured them. They all flout the Emperor's laws, and assert
that there is a rival king, Jesus.' These words caused a great 8
commotion in the mob, which affected the magistrates also.
They bound over Jason and the others, and let them go. 9

As soon as darkness fell, the members of the congrega- 10
tion sent Paul and Silas off to Beroea. On arrival, they
made their way to the synagogue. The Jews here were 11
more liberal-minded than those at Thessalonica: they
received the message with great eagerness, studying the
scriptures every day to see whether it was as they said.
Many of them therefore became believers, and so did a 12
fair number of Greeks, women of standing as well as men.
But when the Thessalonian Jews learned that the word of 13
God had now been proclaimed by Paul in Beroea, they
came on there to stir up trouble and rouse the rabble.
Thereupon the members of the congregation sent Paul 14
off at once to go down to the coast, while Silas and
Timothy both stayed behind. Paul's escort brought him 15
as far as Athens, and came away with instructions for
Silas and Timothy to rejoin him with all speed.

* It is striking to note during the next two chapters the inci-
dents which Luke selects for comment. It need not be supposed
that nothing further happened on the way beyond the events
discussed. As in his Gospel, the whole story cannot be told;
he must select those happenings which most clearly indicate
the progress of the Holy Spirit. No opposition, no persecution
could halt the purpose of God.

 1. *Amphipolis*, *Apollonia* and *Thessalonica* were all on the
Via Egnatia, approximately equidistant from one another,

as was Amphipolis from Philippi—the whole distance being about 100 miles. No details are given of Paul's work in the first two towns, perhaps because he merely passed through them or because there was no nucleus of Jews with whom he could begin. Thessalonica was the capital of Macedonia and ruled by politarchs (verse 6). It had a Jewish community and a synagogue.

2–3. *Following his usual practice Paul went to their meetings.* For three sabbaths Paul expounded the scriptures to prove that Jesus was the Messiah.

4. The result was the conversion of some Jews, *a great number* of Greek 'God-fearers' and *a good many influential women*. Some manuscripts read the latter as 'a good many wives of leading men'.

5–9. The riot. The Jews' ability in stirring up the mob is in line with their efforts in Jerusalem at the martyrdom of Jesus (Luke 23: 18) and of Stephen (7: 57). They were infuriated at not being able to find Paul and Silas and so attacked the house of Jason, who was presumably their host, as Lydia had been in Philippi. In the latter city anti-Jewish feeling had been utilized against Paul and Silas by the slave-girl's owners. Here the Jews themselves—a much larger community (see note on 16: 13)—brought about the hostility by stirring up what is presumably a gentile mob.

5. *the town assembly*: the N.E.B. translation implies a regular court. The Greek word, 'people', might mean the crowd.

6. *the magistrates*: politarchs, the regular title for the city authorities in Macedonia, found on many inscriptions.

7. *there is a rival king*: the charge was treason (cf. Jesus, Luke 23: 2). It is difficult to say how far the sentence, 'the men who have made trouble all over the world have now come here' (verse 6), indicates the strength of the Christian mission or merely the exaggeration of the mob. It was certainly becoming a rallying shout for the opposition. In 1 Thess. 2: 14 the inference is that the Christians were persecuted by their own countrymen. Here the instigation, at least, came from the Jews.

9. *They bound over Jason and the others,* presumably not to admit Paul again into the city. Hence the apostle's comment in 1 Thess. 2: 18, 'So we did propose to come to Thessalonica ...but Satan thwarted us'. For the sake of Jason and his friends Paul could not return.

10–15. *Beroea.* Paul's party escaped from Thessalonica by night and turned south from the Via Egnatia to Beroea.

10–11. The mission began in the usual way in the synagogue, and this time the Jews were willing to consider Paul's message by *studying the scriptures every day to see whether it was as they said.*

12–13. The result was pleasing until the Thessalonian Jews came the 40-odd miles to renew the attack.

14–15. It seems obvious that Paul's friends sent him in advance by sea to Athens, while Silas and Timothy stayed behind to organize the church. Some manuscripts insert that Paul went by land through Thessaly but was unable to preach there. On arrival in Athens he sent for Silas and Timothy to rejoin him as soon as possible. According to 18: 5 they in fact rejoined him in Corinth but there is evidence from Paul's letters that Timothy at least came to Athens and was sent back again from there to encourage the Thessalonians 'to stand firm for the faith' (1 Thess. 3: 2). *

PART I—TO ATHENS: (*b*) IN THE CITY

Now while Paul was waiting for them at Athens he was 16 exasperated to see how the city was full of idols. So he 17 argued in the synagogue with the Jews and gentile worshippers, and also in the city square every day with casual passers-by. And some of the Epicurean and Stoic philo- 18 sophers joined issue with him. Some said, 'What can this charlatan be trying to say?'; others, 'He would appear to be a propagandist for foreign deities'—this because he was preaching about Jesus and Resurrection. So they took 19

him and brought him before the Court of Areopagus and said, 'May we know what this new doctrine is that you
20 propound? You are introducing ideas that sound strange to us, and we should like to know what they mean.'
21 (Now the Athenians in general and the foreigners there had no time for anything but talking or hearing about the latest novelty.)

22 Then Paul stood up before the Court of Areopagus and said: 'Men of Athens, I see that in everything that con-
23 cerns religion you are uncommonly scrupulous. For as I was going round looking at the objects of your worship, I noticed among other things an altar bearing the inscription "To an Unknown God". What you worship but do not know—this is what I now proclaim.

24 'The God who created the world and everything in it, and who is Lord of heaven and earth, does not live in
25 shrines made by men. It is not because he lacks anything that he accepts service at men's hands, for he is himself the
26 universal giver of life and breath and all else. He created every race of men of one stock, to inhabit the whole earth's surface. He fixed the epochs of their history and
27 the limits of their territory. They were to seek God, and, it might be, touch and find him; though indeed he is not
28 far from each one of us, for in him we live and move, in him we exist; as some of your own poets have said,
29 "We are also his offspring." As God's offspring, then, we ought not to suppose that the deity is like an image in gold or silver or stone, shaped by human craftsmanship
30 and design. As for the times of ignorance, God has over-looked them; but now he commands mankind, all men
31 everywhere, to repent, because he has fixed the day on

which he will have the world judged, and justly judged, by a man of his choosing; of this he has given assurance to all by raising him from the dead.'

When they heard about the raising of the dead, some 32 scoffed; and others said, 'We will hear you on this subject some other time.' And so Paul left the assembly. How- 33,34 ever, some men joined him and became believers, including Dionysius, a member of the Court of Areopagus; also a woman named Damaris, and others besides.

✻ The importance of Paul's visit to Athens can be over-emphasized. The city was no longer outstanding politically nor as the centre of Greek culture. Nonetheless, this was the first time that Paul had to present the Christian message to such a highly critical Greek audience.

16. This verse seems to indicate that Paul took stock of his surroundings before he began, and *he was exasperated to see how the city was full of idols.*

17. He began in the usual way by arguing with Jews and 'God-fearers' in the synagogue but also, as a strolling philosopher, by discussing, as Socrates had done, in the market-place (*agora*).

18. It would have been interesting to know what *the Epicurean and Stoic philosophers* put forward in the discussion. Epicureanism was founded by Epicurus (342-270 B.C.) who taught that the senses provided the source of all truth. He reasserted Democritus' teaching that all things were made and destroyed by the free coming together and separation of atoms. He thereby denied immortality. He did not deny the existence of gods but taught that they had no part in the affairs of men. He regarded prudence as the best means of attaining happiness through the practice of virtue. The later use of the adjective to mean 'devoted to pleasure' represents a degradation of the real essence of his teaching. Stoicism was founded in Athens by Zeno of Citium (335-263 B.C.). To the

Stoics God is the power which created and sustains the natural world. He reveals himself through the divine reason or logos in the order and beauty of the world. The more a man lives in accordance with this divine reason the wiser, and thus the better, he becomes. Stoic acceptance of the laws of nature and of conscience and the practice that resulted from Stoic teaching had a very beneficial effect on the ancient world. The word 'stoic' is derived from the stoa (porch or colonnade) where Zeno taught in Athens.

charlatan: literally, 'a seed-picker', i.e. a bird pecking grain and so a scavenger, and thus *charlatan* here exactly expresses the idea of someone with a pretence of knowledge, retailing secondhand ideas.

a propagandist for foreign deities: a similar charge was brought against Socrates. The Epicureans would oppose the teaching on resurrection.

19. *the Court of Areopagus*: this translation in the N.E.B. is more likely than *Areios pagos*: the hill of Ares or Mars, near the Acropolis on the west side, where the court originally met. Paul was brought before the Court more for an inquiry than to answer for some offence. The Areopagus was an ancient and influential body which at this time was probably concerned with education and culture, with an oversight of all lecturing in the city. The inquiry probably took place in public in the Stoa Basileios or colonnade in the market-place rather than on Mars' Hill itself.

19–21. It was a polite invitation, and such discussions were obviously enjoyed by all in Athens, both residents and visitors. Any novel idea was worth examining.

22–31. The Speech. As a first challenge to pagan philosophy, Paul's speech may not have been as successful as he had hoped, but it was certainly not the failure some commentators have implied. Paul carefully avoids the reference to scriptural evidence that he might have used in the synagogue and starts from a visible example. Through the evidence of natural theology, he sees man as God's ultimate creation,

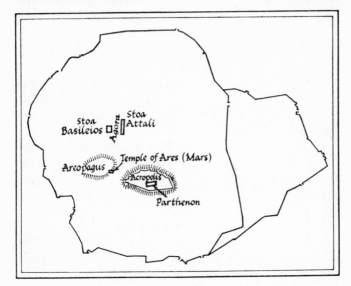

Athens

and with this conception the pagan poets themselves agree. *As God's offspring, then, we ought not to suppose that the deity is like an image in gold or silver or stone.* Then he throws down the challenge to repentance, before the world is judged by the man whom God has chosen. The proof of his choice is made clear *to all by raising him from the dead.*

23. *an altar bearing the inscription 'To an Unknown God'.* Although an altar dedicated to an unknown god has been found on the Palatine in Rome, no similar inscription has yet been discovered in Athens and references by Pausanias, Philostratus and other writers to altars to unknown gods (plural) may merely refer to altars set up without any normal dedication. Nevertheless, Paul's discovery of this altar in the city gave him an excellent beginning for his address.

24. *does not live in shrines made by men* is reminiscent of Solomon's prayer 'heaven and the heaven of heavens cannot

contain thee; how much less this house that I have builded!'
(1 Kings 8: 27)—and of Stephen's speech before the Sanhedrin
(7: 48), where the references are, of course, to the Temple.

24–6. The same idea is expressed in Ps. 50: 12, 'For the
world is mine, and the fulness thereof'. God as the creator of
the world and everything in it would appeal to the Stoics, and
the fact that he *lacks* nothing and is independent of men would
find an echo in Epicurean philosophy.

He fixed the epochs of their history is a better translation than
'fixed the ordered seasons' (N.E.B. footnote): it indicates
God's revelation through human history.

28. '*We are also his offspring*' is a quotation from the Stoic
poet, Aratus of Soli in Cilicia, from his *Phaenomena* 5—a further
indication of Paul's skill in using his material to suit his
audience. A ninth-century commentary by Isho'dad of Merv
gives this passage as a quotation from Aratus and *for in him we
live and move, in him we exist* as one from 'Minos'. With the
latter passage he includes Titus 1: 12, 'Cretans were always
liars, vicious brutes, lazy gluttons'. Clement of Alexandria
(*c.* 150–*c.* 215) ascribes the quotation in Titus to an epic by
Epimenides and thus it has been assumed that both came from
this source. It is more likely that Isho'dad's 'Minos' poem is
by an unknown author.

30. *As for the times of ignorance, God has overlooked them.*
Although God revealed himself in the natural world, men
remained ignorant of his true nature; yet God overlooks this
ignorance in his grace. A similar line of thought is apparent
in Rom. 1: 18–23, but with a different emphasis. Now, *all
men everywhere* are *to repent* before judgement comes.

32–4. The result. How successful was this speech? Some
would write it off as a failure and refer to 1 Cor. 2: 3 where
Paul speaks of his arrival from Athens 'weak, as I was then,
nervous and shaking with fear', resolved in Corinth to declare
the 'truth of God without display of fine words or wisdom'
(1 Cor. 2: 1). Others would say that such a philosophical
address was clearly not Paul's forte. But the evidence of these

concluding verses is quite the contrary. Some did scoff. The
Epicureans were certain to do so *when they heard about the
raising of the dead.* There is no reason to suppose, however, that
the request from others for more discussion later was not
honest. Amongst the men who were converted was *Dionysius,
a member of the Court of Areopagus*; and amongst the women,
Damaris. It was a sound beginning in what might have been
completely unfertile territory; but it must be admitted that
no church appears to have resulted from his efforts, as it did
in other places, even Philippi.

Dionysius, bishop of Corinth (*c.* A.D. 170), calls Dionysius
the Areopagite the first bishop of the church at Athens. ✶

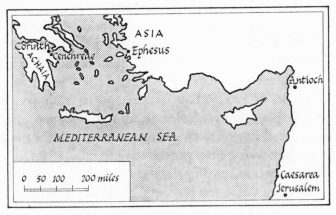

The return to Antioch

PART II—CORINTH AND HOME

After this he left Athens and went to Corinth. There he **18** 1, 2
fell in with a Jew named Aquila, a native of Pontus, and
his wife Priscilla; he had recently arrived from Italy because Claudius had issued an edict that all Jews should
leave Rome. Paul approached them and, because he was 3

of the same trade, he made his home with them, and they
4 carried on business together; they were tent-makers. He
also held discussions in the synagogue Sabbath by Sabbath,
trying to convince both Jews and pagans.

5   Then Silas and Timothy came down from Macedonia,
and Paul devoted himself entirely to preaching, affirming
6 before the Jews that the Messiah was Jesus. But when they
opposed him and resorted to abuse, he shook out the skirts
of his cloak and said to them, 'Your blood be on your
own heads! My conscience is clear; now I shall go to the
7 Gentiles.' With that he left, and went to the house of a
worshipper of God named Titius Justus, who lived next
8 door to the synagogue. Crispus, who held office in the
synagogue, now became a believer in the Lord, with all
his household; and a number of Corinthians listened and
9 believed, and were baptized. One night in a vision the
Lord said to Paul, 'Have no fear: go on with your
10 preaching and do not be silenced, for I am with you and
no one shall attempt to do you harm; and there are many
11 in this city who are my people.' So he settled down for
eighteen months, teaching the word of God among them.
12   But when Gallio was proconsul of Achaia, the Jews set
13 upon Paul in a body and brought him into court. 'This
man', they said, 'is inducing people to worship God in
14 ways that are against the law.' Paul was just about to
speak when Gallio said to them, 'If it had been a question
of crime or grave misdemeanour, I should, of course, have
15 given you Jews a patient hearing, but if it is some bickering
about words and names and your Jewish law, you may
see to it yourselves; I have no mind to be a judge of these
16,17 matters.' And he had them ejected from the court. Then

there was a general attack on Sosthenes, who held office
in the synagogue, and they gave him a beating in full
view of the bench. But all this left Gallio quite uncon-
cerned.

Paul stayed on for some time, and then took leave of 18
the brotherhood and set sail for Syria, accompanied by
Priscilla and Aquila. At Cenchreae he had his hair cut off,
because he was under a vow. When they reached Ephesus 19
he parted from them and went himself into the synagogue,
where he held a discussion with the Jews. He was asked 20
to stay longer, but declined and set out from Ephesus, 21
saying, as he took leave of them, 'I shall come back to
you if it is God's will.' On landing at Caesarea, he went 22
up and paid his respects to the church, and then went down
to Antioch.

✻ The importance of Corinth for the spread of the Christian
gospel is apparent from this visit of Paul to the city and from
his subsequent letters. The work there posed many questions.
Like all seaports, the city was of very mixed population; it had
a strong Jewish element. It was well known for its immorality
and vice. It was important politically as the seat of the Roman
proconsul since A.D. 44. Paul's stay there of nearly two years
(verses 11 and 18) gave him a very distinctive place in the
Corinthian church (1 Cor. 1: 12; 3: 5–6); so distinctive that
there was the danger of his acquiring a private following.
Corinth was a challenge to Paul and his companions, as
Athens had been in a different way. The business world is just
as hard a nut to crack as the intellectual, and few men are
competent to deal with both. It is noteworthy that so highly
educated a man as Paul dealt with Corinth so effectively.

Again Luke produces the quick change reminiscent of the
television screen. At one moment we see Paul leaving the
dignified court of the Areopagus in Athens in company with

Dionysius and Damaris; the next he is doing a business deal with an Asiatic Jew and his wife, lately come from Rome to Corinth. It sheds a revealing light on the man as well as on the church at work.

2. *a Jew named Aquila, a native of Pontus, and his wife Priscilla*: these two obviously become close friends of Paul from the greetings he sends to them in Rom. 16: 3 and 2 Tim. 4: 19 or from them in 1 Cor. 16: 19. In each case Priscilla is known as Prisca; was it a pet-name? Aquila's home was in Pontus in Asia Minor, but he and his wife had recently been resident in Italy. Orosius, a fifth-century historian and friend of Augustine, gives the date of the edict under which they had been expelled as the ninth year of Claudius, i.e. A.D. 49–50. The Roman historian Suetonius (*c.* 75–160), secretary to the emperor Hadrian, wrote in his 'Life of Claudius' (xxv. 4): 'Since the Jews constantly made disturbances at the instigation of Chrestus, he (Claudius) expelled them from Rome.' Chrestus may, of course, be the name of a Jewish revolutionary, but it seems likely that it represents a confusion with Christ. The passage may well refer to the advent of Christianity in Rome and trouble with the Jews as a result, leading to Claudius' edict. It is not necessary to assume that the expulsion referred to by Suetonius resulted from the edict noted by Orosius but the date A.D. 49–50 seems to fit in well with Gallio's pro-consulship (see below verse 12). There is no reason to suppose that Aquila and Priscilla were Christians before they met Paul.

3. Paul often referred to his ability to earn his own living by manual work rather than be a burden to the new churches; e.g. in his address to the elders of Ephesus at Miletus (20: 34) and to the Corinthians themselves (1 Cor. 4: 12).

tent-makers or leather-workers, i.e. makers of felted cloth for tents.

4. Once again the mission began in the synagogue amongst Jews and 'God-fearers'.

5. Silas and Timothy now return from Macedonia, and Timothy brings 'good news of your faith and love' from

Thessalonica (1 Thess. 3: 6). Paul's letters to the Thessalonians were written at this time.

5-6. The mission follows the usual pattern: Jews first and, on their rejection of the message, Gentiles (cf. at Pisidian Antioch, 'we now turn to the Gentiles', 13: 46).

he shook out the skirts of his cloak: as a sign of rejection. See Neh. 5: 13, 'I shook out my lap, and said, So God shake out every man from his house...even thus be he shaken out, and emptied'. For another similar symbolic action see 13: 51, 'So they shook the dust off their feet in protest against them'.

Your blood be on your own heads! Cf. the cry of the mob to Pilate: 'His blood be on us, and on our children' (Matt. 27: 25).

7-8. The establishment of the Christian church at the house of a 'God-fearer' next door to the synagogue would seem a bold move. It argues that there were considerable sympathetic elements among the Jews, and that Paul was far from abandoning hope for his compatriots (cf. Rom. 11). His optimism was justified, especially as one of the officials of the synagogue itself *became a believer in the Lord, with all his household*.

Titius Justus: the N.E.B. reading is probably more correct than Titus.

Crispus: Paul himself baptized Crispus (1 Cor. 1: 14). This was exceptional in Corinth; Paul baptized few converts there.

9-11. Paul's vision and his subsequent eighteen months' work in the city indicate a period of steady growth.

12. The summons of Paul before Gallio was probably soon after the latter's appointment (cf. Paul's trial before Festus later, 25: 1-2). Junius Annaeus *Gallio* was the brother of the philosopher Seneca, and uncle of the poet Lucan. His name appears in an inscription found at Delphi in 1905, which contains a decision of the emperor, Claudius, on a matter submitted to him by Gallio when proconsul of Achaia in A.D. 51-2. This is an important date in fixing New Testament chronology.

13-15. The charge is very indefinite and in Gallio's eyes

clearly irrelevant. He refused Paul permission to speak and dismissed the case as *some bickering about words and names and your Jewish law*. But for Paul this was a triumph, and Luke clearly wishes it so to be understood. The Roman authorities had refused to take action against him. One wonders whether the events which had taken place at Philippi and had been so humiliating to the magistrates had been reported in Corinth (16: 35-40).

17. *Sosthenes*: it seems unlikely that this is the man later associated with Paul in 1 Cor. 1: 1. He was probably the synagogue official, perhaps the one who had replaced Crispus and had led the attack on Paul. Gallio's unconcern at the action of the mob in beating up Sosthenes must have been a final triumph for Paul and his supporters. The Jewish faction had failed.

18-22. The journey home to Syrian Antioch.

The conclusion of this second extended journey, during which firm bridgeheads had been established in Europe at Philippi, Thessalonica, Athens and Corinth, is hurried. There is no need to assume difficulties from the account. Luke's main purposes have been accomplished in narrating the story of what happened at these four main centres. The remainder of the trip is, therefore, merely a timetable.

18. The party, accompanied by Priscilla and Aquila, leaves from Cenchreae, the eastern port across the isthmus from Corinth, on the first stage of the journey to Syria.

he had his hair cut off, because he was under a vow: presumably a Nazirite (one 'consecrated' to God) vow (Num. 6: 18). This was either the end of a vow, perhaps of thanksgiving for the mission, or the beginning of one, to be redeemed in Jerusalem. Luke uses it to indicate Paul's adherence to Jewish customs (cf. the similar vow in 21: 23-6), that as a Jew he accepted the Law (see above: the note on Timothy's circumcision, 16: 1-5).

19-21. *Ephesus*: presumably while changing ships or waiting for cargo to be discharged Paul visited the local synagogue.

Priscilla and Aquila remained in Ephesus (verse 26), while
Paul promised to return later, as he did in chapter 19.

22. After the landing at Caesarea Luke implies a visit to
Jerusalem, presumably to complete the vow. *Went up* and
went down suggest this visit to the capital, but no place is
mentioned. Antioch marked the completion of the round
trip this time as it had done before. ✶

AN INTERLUDE

After spending some time there, he set out again and 23
made a journey through the Galatian country and on
through Phrygia, bringing new strength to all the converts.

✶ This verse, though clearly attached to the last section in
the N.E.B., is the link with Paul's long stay in Ephesus. The
traditional division into three 'missionary journeys' was not
in Luke's mind at all. The expedition before the council of
Jerusalem was one entity and so, too, was the whole section
from the departure from Antioch in 15: 36–41 to the arrival
in Jerusalem in 21: 17–26, as indicated in the N.E.B. This
journey through Asia Minor was to bring *new strength to all
the converts*, whether or not *the Galatian country* means the
whole province of Galatia, north and south, or simply the
towns of 'the first journey' (see note on 16: 6). ✶

EPHESUS: (*a*) STEADY PROGRESS

Now there arrived at Ephesus a Jew named Apollos, an 24
Alexandrian by birth, an eloquent man, powerful in his
use of the scriptures. He had been instructed in the way of 25
the Lord and was full of spiritual fervour; and in his dis-
courses he taught accurately the facts about Jesus, though
he knew only John's baptism. He now began to speak 26

Paul in Ephesus

boldly in the synagogue, where Priscilla and Aquila heard him; they took him in hand and expounded the new way to him in greater detail. Finding that he wished 27 to go across to Achaia, the brotherhood gave him their support, and wrote to the congregation there to make him welcome. From the time of his arrival, he was very helpful to those who had by God's grace become believers; for he was indefatigable in confuting the Jews, 28 demonstrating publicly from the scriptures that the Messiah is Jesus.

While Apollos was at Corinth, Paul travelled through **19** the inland regions till he came to Ephesus. There he found a number of converts, to whom he said, 'Did you receive 2 the Holy Spirit when you became believers?' 'No,' they replied, 'we have not even heard that there is a Holy Spirit.' He said, 'Then what baptism were you given?' 3 'John's baptism', they answered. Paul then said, 'The 4 baptism that John gave was a baptism in token of repentance, and he told the people to put their trust in one who was to come after him, that is, in Jesus.' On hearing 5 this they were baptized into the name of the Lord Jesus; and when Paul had laid his hands on them, the Holy 6 Spirit came upon them and they spoke in tongues of ecstasy and prophesied. Altogether they were about a 7 dozen men.

During the next three months he attended the synagogue 8 and, using argument and persuasion, spoke boldly and freely about the kingdom of God. But when some proved 9 obdurate and would not believe, speaking evil of the new way before the whole congregation, he left them, withdrew his converts, and continued to hold discussions daily

10 in the lecture-hall of Tyrannus. This went on for two
years, with the result that the whole population of the
province of Asia, both Jews and pagans, heard the word
11 of the Lord. And through Paul God worked miracles of
12 an unusual kind: when handkerchiefs and scarves which
had been in contact with his skin were carried to the sick,
they were rid of their diseases and the evil spirits came
out of them.

13 But some strolling Jewish exorcists tried their hand at
using the name of the Lord Jesus on those possessed by
evil spirits; they would say, 'I adjure you by Jesus whom
14 Paul proclaims.' There were seven sons of Sceva, a Jewish
15 chief priest, who were using this method, when the evil
spirit answered back and said, 'Jesus I acknowledge, and
16 I know about Paul, but who are you?' And the man with
the evil spirit flew at them, overpowered them all, and
handled them with such violence that they ran out of the
17 house stripped and battered. This became known to every-
body in Ephesus, whether Jew or pagan; they were all
awestruck, and the name of the Lord Jesus gained in
18 honour. Moreover many of those who had become believers came and openly confessed that they had been
19 using magical spells. And a good many of those who
formerly practised magic collected their books and burnt
them publicly. The total value was reckoned up and it
20 came to fifty thousand pieces of silver. In such ways the
word of the Lord showed its power, spreading more and
more widely and effectively.

21 When things had reached this stage, Paul made up his
mind to visit Macedonia and Achaia and then go on to
Jerusalem; and he said, 'After I have been there, I must

see Rome also.' So he sent two of his assistants, Timothy 22
and Erastus, to Macedonia, while he himself stayed some
time longer in the province of Asia.

✻ 24–8. *Apollos*: this man was clearly of considerable importance in the story of the Way, especially in Corinth, where
his standing was so high that a party was formed in his name
on a par with those of Peter and Paul (1 Cor. 1: 12). Luke's
introduction of him is, therefore, more complete than usual:
a Jew ..., *an Alexandrian by birth*, *an eloquent* (or, as the N.E.B.
footnote, 'learned') *man*, *powerful in his use of the scriptures.*
Alexandria was famous at this time for its blending of Judaism
with hellenistic philosophy. Apollos *had been instructed in the
way of the Lord* and enthusiastically and accurately taught *the
facts about Jesus* (or 'the Lord' in some manuscripts). His one
defect was that *he knew only John's baptism* (i.e. a baptism of
repentance, not into the name of Jesus, to become his possession).

26. When Aquila and Priscilla heard Apollos in the synagogue, *they took him in hand* and explained the full implications
of *the new way* (or, as the N.E.B. footnote, 'the way of God').
The word *new* is not in the Greek (see above, 9: 2).

27. *the brotherhood*: a church in Ephesus had grown up,
probably through the efforts of Priscilla, Aquila and Apollos,
and its members now sent a commendatory letter to the church
in *Achaia* (presumably Corinth) to introduce Apollos. The
practice of sending such letters of introduction is referred to
in 2 Cor. 3: 1.

27–8. Apollos' deep knowledge of the scriptures made him
a great help to the Corinthian church in proving to the Jews
the Messiahship of Jesus.

Martin Luther suggested that Apollos wrote A Letter to
Hebrews. Perhaps it emanated from the group at Ephesus of
which Priscilla was the most prominent member. Her name
sometimes appears before that of her husband, especially in
connexion with Ephesus (verses 18 and 26). The seventeenth-

century book of devotion *The Whole Duty of Man*, first published about 1658, may be cited as a parallel, for it too is anonymous and may well have originated among a pious group worshipping together during the English Puritan Revolution.

19: 1–7. Paul arrives in Ephesus. During Apollos' absence in Corinth Paul reached Ephesus by the overland route from Phrygia and found there the beginnings of a Christian church.

1. *converts*: the Greek, 'disciples', has this meaning in Acts.

2–5. Like Apollos, these converts 'knew only John's baptism' (18: 25). They had not heard of the gift of the Spirit at Pentecost. Their position was regularized by baptism *into the name of the Lord Jesus*, i.e. into his possession.

6. *when Paul had laid his hands on them, the Holy Spirit came upon them*, in the same way as it had on the Samaritans after Peter and John had laid on their hands (8: 17).

they spoke in tongues of ecstasy and prophesied is reminiscent of the gift of the Spirit to Cornelius and his friends (10: 46) before their baptism.

7. *about a dozen men*: clearly a rough figure. There seems no purpose in trying to equate the figure twelve with the number of apostles, or these events at Ephesus with those at Jerusalem at Pentecost, but Luke may have regarded it as a parallel in the formation of the church at Ephesus.

8–12. The beginning of Paul's work in the city.

The usual pattern is followed: first, discussion in the synagogue followed by opposition from some members, then freer exposition of the Way elsewhere.

9. *lecture-hall of Tyrannus*: i.e. owned or used by a philosopher named Tyrannus. One manuscript adds 'from the fifth to the tenth hours', 11 a.m. to 4 p.m., the middle of the day, when Tyrannus would not be using it himself, but would be taking the normal siesta.

10. *two years*: Paul's stay in Ephesus was probably even longer, if the 'three months' of verse 8 and 'some time longer' in verse 22 are added.

the province of Asia: Ephesus was the capital of the province.

During this period the churches of Laodicea, Colossae and Hierapolis must have been established, though not necessarily by Paul himself (Col. 2: 1; 4: 13), and probably the other churches named in the Book of Revelation (1: 11). Nothing is said here of the Corinthian Letters, with which Paul was engaged at this time (1 Cor. 16: 8–9, 'I shall remain at Ephesus until Whitsuntide, for a great opportunity has opened for effective work, and there is much opposition').

11–12. Paul continues the work of healing as Stephen had done (6: 8). The idea that Paul's healing power was contagious and conveyed by *handkerchiefs and scarves* is reminiscent of Jesus' cloak (Luke 8: 44) and Peter's shadow (5: 15). These parallels, with those in the next few verses, again show that in Luke's view as the church grows the same patterns recur (see note above on 16: 40 and conclusion, pp. 223–7).

13–20. Another clash with magic. This time it is with Jewish exorcism, but it resembles the encounters with Simon (8: 9–13) and Elymas (13: 6–12).

13. The use of Jesus' name in this way was known in his own day (Luke 9: 49), but the sons of Sceva were trying to use the name of Jesus without being his followers in *any* sense.

14. *Sceva*: nothing is known of him; perhaps he came from an important priestly family.

16. *overpowered them all*: literally, 'both of them', but used in a wider sense.

17. The event naturally enhanced the reputation of the church (cf. the story of Ananias and Sapphira 5: 1–12).

18–20. Converts who had retained their magical practices now gave them up, realizing that they were incompatible with Christianity. Their books of incantations were burnt and valued at 50,000 drachmas (very roughly a year's salary for a fairly well-paid man). This seems a large amount but it is difficult to determine how much books cost in those days and to evaluate them in modern currency.

21–2. The next stage. Paul plans a visit to Greece, then Jerusalem and, at last, Rome.

21. *made up his mind*: the N.E.B. footnote, 'led by the Spirit, resolved', indicates his feeling of spiritual guidance.

22. The visit of *Timothy and Erastus, to Macedonia* may have been in connexion with Paul's Corinthian correspondence (1 Cor. 4: 17, 'That is the very reason why I have sent Timothy'). The name Erastus appears twice more in the New Testament: Rom. 16: 23 and 2 Tim. 4: 20, but may not refer to the same man. ✲

EPHESUS: (*b*) THE RIOT

23 Now about that time, the Christian movement gave rise
24 to a serious disturbance. There was a man named Demetrius, a silversmith who made silver shrines of Diana
and provided a great deal of employment for the crafts-
25 men. He called a meeting of these men and the workers
in allied trades, and addressed them. 'Men,' he said, 'you
know that our high standard of living depends on this
26 industry. And you see and hear how this fellow Paul with
his propaganda has perverted crowds of people, not only
at Ephesus but also in practically the whole of the province of Asia. He is telling them that gods made by
27 human hands are not gods at all. There is danger for us
here; it is not only that our line of business will be discredited, but also that the sanctuary of the great goddess
Diana will cease to command respect; and then it will not
be long before she who is worshipped by all Asia and the
civilized world is brought down from her divine pre-
eminence.'

28 When they heard this they were roused to fury and
29 shouted, 'Great is Diana of the Ephesians!' The whole
city was in confusion; they seized Paul's travelling-companions, the Macedonians Gaius and Aristarchus, and

made a concerted rush with them into the theatre. Paul 30
wanted to appear before the assembly but the other
Christians would not let him. Even some of the dig- 31
nitaries of the province, who were friendly towards him,
sent and urged him not to venture into the theatre.
Meanwhile some were shouting one thing, some another; 32
for the assembly was in confusion and most of them did
not know what they had all come for. But some of the 33
crowd explained the trouble to Alexander, whom the
Jews had pushed to the front, and he, motioning for
silence, attempted to make a defence before the assembly.
But when they recognized that he was a Jew, a single cry 34
arose from them all: for about two hours they kept on
shouting, 'Great is Diana of the Ephesians!'

The town clerk, however, quieted the crowd. 'Men of 35
Ephesus,' he said, 'all the world knows that our city of
Ephesus is temple-warden of the great Diana and of that
symbol of her which fell from heaven. Since these facts 36
are beyond dispute, your proper course is to keep quiet
and do nothing rash. These men whom you have brought 37
here as culprits have committed no sacrilege and uttered
no blasphemy against our goddess. If therefore Demetrius 38
and his craftsmen have a case against anyone, assizes are
held and there are such people as proconsuls; let the parties
bring their charges and countercharges. If, on the other 39
hand, you have some further question to raise, it will be
dealt with in the statutory assembly. We certainly run 40
the risk of being charged with riot for this day's work.
There is no justification for it, and if the issue is raised we
shall be unable to give any explanation of this uproar.'
With that he dismissed the assembly. 41

✲ This is one of the most exciting passages in Acts. Luke exploits to the full his remarkable ability in dramatic writing. There is another galaxy of characters: Demetrius and his colleagues from his own and *allied trades*; *the Macedonians Gaius and Aristarchus*; some *dignitaries of the province*; the Jew, *Alexander*; *the town clerk*, and, above all, that essential to Luke's stories: the fractious, easily-led mob. The setting is the great Ephesian theatre and the roads leading to it. Perhaps the uproar was the culmination of the troubles in Ephesus mentioned in 1 Cor. 15: 32 and 16: 9 and in 2 Cor. 1: 8–11.

24. *silver shrines of Diana*: the Roman name for the Greek 'Artemis', sister of Apollo, but here representing the fertility goddess of Asia Minor, 'the Great Mother'. Her temple at Ephesus was one of the seven wonders of the world. The shrines may have been replicas of Diana's statue.

25–6. The disturbance was the outcome of an economic dispute. Paul, by his preaching against idolatry, was likely to reduce the *standard of living* of Demetrius and his friends, who would lose trade if the worship of Diana was discredited.

27. The fear of disrespect to Diana seems somewhat of an afterthought.

29. The mob takes over, and there is a rush on the great theatre. Of Paul's two friends, whom the crowd captures, *Aristarchus* alone was a Macedonian from Thessalonica (20: 4), unless *Gaius* came from Doberus in Macedonia (as the N.E.B. assumes, with some manuscripts, in 20: 4) and not Derbe in Asia Minor.

31. *the dignitaries of the province*: Asiarchs, representatives of the Asian cities who formed a council to maintain political links with Rome and especially to uphold the cult of Emperor-worship. Their intervention shows again the friendliness of Roman officials to Paul and his companions.

33. *Alexander*: presumably *the Jews...pushed* him *to the front* to explain that they had nothing to do with Paul; all to no purpose. The name appears in 1 Tim. 1: 20 and 2 Tim. 4: 14, but it is unlikely to be the same person.

35–41. The town clerk's control of the crowd is masterly. He was clearly an important official and, as such, respected by the citizens.

35. *temple-warden*: literally, 'temple-sweeper', i.e. guardian, a title given to cities, usually in connexion with Emperor-worship. At Ephesus it was an official title relating to Diana as well.

that symbol...which fell from heaven: probably a meteorite roughly in the form of a woman. Greek, *Diopetes*: fallen from Zeus. Diana was the daughter of Zeus and Leto.

38. *assizes are held and there are such people as proconsuls*: the N.E.B. gives the right interpretation. There was only one proconsul and he presided over the assizes. 'The courts are open, and there are proconsuls' in both the R.V. and R.S.V. suggests a series of courts, each with its own proconsul.

39. *statutory assembly*: i.e. of the local authority, before which a resolution could be brought.

40. *run the risk of being charged with riot*: Rome might well punish the city for such an uproar. ✳

FROM EPHESUS TO GREECE
AND BACK TO MILETUS

When the disturbance had ceased, Paul sent for the **20** disciples and, after encouraging them, said good-bye and set out on his journey to Macedonia. He travelled 2 through those parts of the country, often speaking words of encouragement to the Christians there, and so came into Greece. When he had spent three months there and 3 was on the point of embarking for Syria, a plot was laid against him by the Jews, so he decided to return by way of Macedonia. He was accompanied by Sopater son of 4 Pyrrhus, from Beroea, the Thessalonians Aristarchus and Secundus, Gaius the Doberian and Timothy, and the

Paul in Europe again, and back to Miletus

Asians Tychicus and Trophimus. These went ahead and 5
waited for us at Troas; we ourselves set sail from Philippi 6
after the Passover season, and in five days reached them
at Troas, where we spent a week.

On the Saturday night, in our assembly for the breaking 7
of bread, Paul, who was to leave next day, addressed
them, and went on speaking until midnight. Now there 8
were many lamps in the upper room where we were
assembled; and a youth named Eutychus, who was sitting 9
on the window-ledge, grew more and more sleepy as
Paul went on talking. At last he was completely over-
come by sleep, fell from the third floor to the ground,
and was picked up for dead. Paul went down, threw 10
himself upon him, seizing him in his arms, and said to them,
'Stop this commotion: there is still life in him.' He then 11
went upstairs, broke bread and ate, and after much conversation, which lasted until dawn, he departed. And they 12
took the boy away alive and were immensely comforted.

We went ahead to the ship and sailed for Assos, where 13
we were to take Paul aboard. He had made this arrange-
ment, as he was going to travel by road. When he met 14
us at Assos, we took him aboard and went on to Mitylene.
Next day we sailed from there and arrived opposite 15
Chios, and on the second day we made Samos. On the
following day we reached Miletus. For Paul had decided 16
to pass by Ephesus and so avoid having to spend time in
the province of Asia; he was eager to be in Jerusalem, if
he possibly could, on the day of Pentecost.

* The real conclusion to Paul's Ephesian visit is his address
to 'the elders of the congregation' which took place at Miletus
(see below, verses 17 ff.); but between his departure from

Ephesus and his return to Miletus much happened. The Greek expedition had been planned before the riot (19: 21), and it was clearly opportune that Paul should set out as soon as *the disturbance had ceased*. Some commentators hold the theory that Paul was imprisoned in Ephesus, which would have further delayed his departure. The summary of the ensuing campaign in *Greece* (the word, *Hellas*, occurs only here in the New Testament) resembles that of the journey preceding Paul's arrival in Ephesus (18: 23) and thus by comparison indicates the stress Luke wishes to place on the work in Ephesus itself.

2. We know from 2 Cor. 2: 12–13 that at Troas on this journey Paul was so disturbed by affairs in Corinth and Titus' non-return from there that he was unable to use the opportunities for preaching that appeared and so went on into Macedonia. There he was ill, with 'trouble at every turn, quarrels all round us, forebodings in our heart' (2 Cor. 7: 5). Soon after, however, he was comforted by the arrival of Titus and the good news he brought from Corinth (2 Cor. 7: 6–7). Paul's illness and the recommencement of the 'we-section' in verse 5 suggest that Luke was called in professionally at this point (see note above on 16: 9–10).

3. Paul then went on to Greece and *spent three months there*. During this period he probably wrote the Letter to the Romans and may have travelled to Illyricum (Rom. 15: 19). His principal task was the organization of the collection which he hoped to take to the poor Christians in Jerusalem (Rom. 15: 26). It is noteworthy that Luke does not mention Titus at all and the collection only in passing (24: 17). These details were not relevant to the story Luke was telling.

The Jewish *plot* may have been to kill him at Cenchreae as he was *embarking for Syria* or to steal the collection. Whatever it was, he decided to return by land.

4. Another list of friends, perhaps delegates from the churches to take the collection with Paul to Jerusalem (see note below on 24: 17)—Sopater from Beroea, Aristarchus

(19: 29) and Secundus from Thessalonica, Gaius from Doberus (see note on 19: 29) or Derbe, Timothy from Lystra, Tychicus (Eph. 6: 21 and 2 Tim. 4: 12) and Trophimus (21: 29) from Ephesus.

Some manuscripts add 'as far as Asia'.

5–6. The main party went on to Troas. Paul and Luke (the next 'we-section' begins here) remained at Philippi for the Passover (literally, 'days of Unleavened Bread').

The five-day journey to Troas was a long one compared with the two days in the opposite direction (16: 11).

7–12. *Eutychus*: another dramatic interlude introducing a scene from the church at Troas, of which nothing has so far been said. Luke may well have singled it out from this closely compact story of the return journey in order to provide an account of raising from the dead for Paul to parallel that of Dorcas for Peter (9: 36–43)—(see note above on 19: 11–12 and conclusion pp. 223–7). The N.E.B. softens the miraculous side of the event by the translation *was picked up for dead* (verse 9) instead of the R.V. and R.S.V. 'was taken up dead'.

7. *On the Saturday night*: literally, 'on the first day of the week'. This assumes that Luke is following the Jewish reckoning, with the day beginning at sunset. It seems likely that the church would begin Sunday with *the breaking of bread* rather than end it so, though some commentators suggest that the service at Troas was on Sunday evening, thus using the Roman method of reckoning the day. Sunday was already regarded as a special day for worship (1 Cor. 16: 2; Rev. 1: 10). There is no clear indication whether or not the communion with its address was preceded by the common meal or love-feast.

8. At a later date, there were rumours in some hostile pagan circles that Christians committed atrocities at midnight services (held in darkness). The mention of *many lamps* here shows how baseless such rumours were.

9. A pleasantly human comment on Paul's lengthy discourse and Eutychus' growing sleepiness.

the third floor: an interesting reference to the heights to which house buildings went, as has been revealed in particular by excavations at Ostia, the port of Rome.

10. *there is still life in him*: again reduces the miraculous content.

13–16. Troas to Miletus. Paul went overland to Assos on the southern side of the promontory and there joined his companions who had travelled by sea. After a stop at Mitylene on the island of Lesbos, they skirted the islands of Chios and Samos. Some manuscripts then add that they called at Trogyllium on the mainland before reaching Miletus.

16. Having missed getting to Jerusalem for the Passover by returning via Macedonia, Paul was anxious to get there by Pentecost. ✷

THE ADDRESS AT MILETUS TO THE ELDERS
OF EPHESUS

17 He did, however, send from Miletus to Ephesus and
18 summon the elders of the congregation; and when they joined him, he spoke as follows:

'You know how, from the day that I first set foot in the province of Asia, for the whole time that I was with
19 you, I served the Lord in all humility amid the sorrows and trials that came upon me through the machinations
20 of the Jews. You know that I kept back nothing that was for your good: I delivered the message to you; I taught
21 you, in public and in your homes; with Jews and pagans alike I insisted on repentance before God and trust in our
22 Lord Jesus. And now, as you see, I am on my way to Jerusalem, under the constraint of the Spirit. Of what
23 will befall me there I know nothing, except that in city after city the Holy Spirit assures me that imprisonment
24 and hardships await me. For myself, I set no store by

life; I only want to finish the race, and complete the task which the Lord Jesus assigned to me, of bearing my testimony to the gospel of God's grace.

'One word more: I have gone about among you pro- 25 claiming the Kingdom, but now I know that none of you will see my face again. That being so, I here and now 26 declare that no man's fate can be laid at my door; for 27 I have kept back nothing; I have disclosed to you the whole purpose of God. Keep watch over yourselves and 28 over all the flock of which the Holy Spirit has given you charge, as shepherds of the church of the Lord, which he won for himself by his own blood. I know that when 29 I am gone, savage wolves will come in among you and will not spare the flock. Even from your own body there 30 will be men coming forward who will distort the truth to induce the disciples to break away and follow them. So be on the alert; remember how for three years, night 31 and day, I never ceased to counsel each of you, and how I wept over you.

'And now I commend you to God and to his gracious 32 word, which has power to build you up and give you your heritage among all who are dedicated to him. I have 33 not wanted anyone's money or clothes for myself; you all 34 know that these hands of mine earned enough for the needs of me and my companions. I showed you that it 35 is our duty to help the weak in this way, by hard work, and that we should keep in mind the words of the Lord Jesus, who himself said, "Happiness lies more in giving than in receiving."'

As he finished speaking, he knelt down with them all 36 and prayed. Then there were loud cries of sorrow from 37

them all, as they folded Paul in their arms and kissed him.
38 What distressed them most was his saying that they would
never see his face again. So they escorted him to his ship.

* Paul avoided visiting Ephesus, as it would have meant too
long a stay, but he found time to call the leaders of the church
for a brief farewell at Miletus. He frequently returned to
exhort and confirm the members of the churches he founded,
but this address alone gives some idea of what he said.

Despite all the difficulties that beset him from the Jews, he
taught, *in public and in* their *homes,* to *Jews and pagans alike* the
whole gospel of repentance and faith in Jesus. Now he feels
the compulsion of the Spirit to go on to Jerusalem, anticipating
further persecution. No matter what may happen, he was
determined to complete the task of proclaiming *the gospel of
God's grace.*

As they were to see him no more, and in furtherance of the
entire gospel that he had put before them, he charged them
as shepherds of Christ's flock in Ephesus to protect the church
from enemies who would arise from outside and from inside
their own number. They must keep on the alert and always
remember that for three years he struggled on their behalf in
the city.

Finally he commended them to God and once again
reminded them that he had worked side by side with them to
keep himself and his companions. Thus, by hard work, he
showed them that they should help the weak and keep in
mind Jesus' words: *Happiness lies more in giving than in
receiving.*

22. *under the constraint of the Spirit*: or, as the N.E.B.
footnote, 'under an inner compulsion', literally, 'bound in
the spirit', i.e. by divine command.

28. *shepherds of the church of the Lord* (or some manuscripts,
'God'): R.V. 'bishops'; R.S.V. 'guardians'. The Greek is
episcopoi or 'overseers'. In verse 17 Luke refers to the leaders
of the Ephesian church as 'elders' or *presbyteroi*. The leaders

of the church in Ephesus were all overseers of its worship and work. If the word 'God' is adopted instead of *the Lord*, then the sentence should conclude, as in the N.E.B. footnote, 'by the blood of his Own', i.e. through the death of Christ.

29–30. The precise dangers Paul has in mind are false teaching and division.

32. *build you up and give you your heritage*: i.e. the Christians of Ephesus will be built into the whole church of Christ and be given their inheritance in it.

35. The quotation is not to be found in the Gospels but may well have been handed down orally. It is used in the manner of an Old Testament 'proof-text' from Jesus' own words and thus is an indication of the way in which such quotations would be used in early sermons. It is also evidence of a rich tradition surviving outside the Gospels.

36–8. After Paul had spoken, they prayed together and with much distress *escorted him to his ship*. ✳

TO JERUSALEM

When we had parted from them and set sail, we made **21** a straight run and came to Cos; next day to Rhodes, and thence to Patara. There we found a ship bound for 2 Phoenicia, so we went aboard and sailed in her. We came 3 in sight of Cyprus, and leaving it on our port beam, we continued our voyage to Syria, and put in at Tyre, for there the ship was to unload her cargo. We went and 4 found the disciples and stayed there a week; and they, warned by the Spirit, urged Paul to abandon his visit to Jerusalem. But when our time ashore was ended, we left 5 and continued our journey; and they and their wives and children all escorted us out of the city. We knelt down on the beach and prayed, then bade each other good-bye; 6 we went aboard, and they returned home.

7   We made the passage from Tyre and reached Ptolemais,
where we greeted the brotherhood and spent one day
8 with them. Next day we left and came to Caesarea. We
went to the home of Philip the evangelist, who was one
9 of the Seven, and stayed with him. He had four unmarried daughters, who possessed the gift of prophecy.

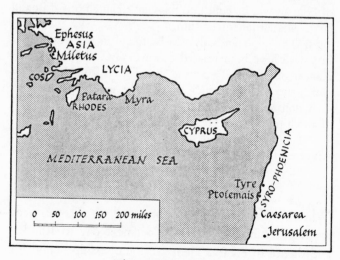

The return to Jerusalem

10 When we had been there several days, a prophet named
11 Agabus arrived from Judaea. He came to us, took Paul's
belt, bound his own feet and hands with it, and said,
'These are the words of the Holy Spirit: Thus will the
Jews in Jerusalem bind the man to whom this belt belongs,
12 and hand him over to the Gentiles.' When we heard this,
we and the local people begged and implored Paul to
13 abandon his visit to Jerusalem. Then Paul gave his answer:
'Why all these tears? Why are you trying to weaken

174

my resolution? For my part I am ready not merely to
be bound but even to die for the name of the Lord Jesus.'
So, as he would not be persuaded, we gave up and said, 14
'The Lord's will be done.'

At the end of our stay we packed our baggage and took 15
the road up to Jerusalem. Some of the disciples from 16
Caesarea came along with us, bringing a certain Mnason
of Cyprus, a Christian from the early days, with whom
we were to lodge. So we reached Jerusalem, where the 17
brotherhood welcomed us gladly.

Next day Paul paid a visit to James; we were with him, 18
and all the elders attended. He greeted them, and then 19
described in detail all that God had done among the
Gentiles through his ministry. When they heard this, they 20
gave praise to God. Then they said to Paul: 'You see,
brother, how many thousands of converts we have among
the Jews, all of them staunch upholders of the Law. Now 21
they have been given certain information about you: it is
said that you teach all the Jews in the gentile world to
turn their backs on Moses, telling them to give up circumcising their children and following our way of life.
What is the position, then? They are sure to hear that 22
you have arrived. You must therefore do as we tell you. 23
We have four men here who are under a vow; take them 24
with you and go through the ritual of purification with
them, paying their expenses, after which they may shave
their heads. Then everyone will know that there is nothing
in the stories they were told about you, but that you are
a practising Jew and keep the Law yourself. As for the 25
gentile converts, we sent them our decision that they must
abstain from meat that has been offered to idols, from

blood, from anything that has been strangled, and from
26 fornication.' So Paul took the four men, and next day,
after going through the ritual of purification with them,
he went into the temple to give notice of the date when
the period of purification would end and the offering be
made for each one of them.

* 1–6. Stage 1: To Tyre. The voyage was a straightforward
one via the islands of Cos and Rhodes, and then via Patara on
the mainland in Lycia. Some manuscripts add a call at Myra,
farther east along the coast, before the ship bound for Phoenicia
was boarded. Passing *in sight of Cyprus...on our port beam*
(literally, 'the left-hand'), they reached Tyre where the cargo
was to be unloaded.

4. They stayed for a week with Christian converts or
disciples, who, with divine premonition, warned Paul of
danger if he went on to Jerusalem.

5–6. After prayer on the beach the Tyrians and their families
bade Paul's party farewell, as they went on board again.

7–14. Stage 2: To Caesarea. This journey was accomplished in two sections, by sea to Ptolemais (the modern Acre)
and then probably again by sea to Caesarea. Excavations at
both these places reveal interesting remains of those days.

8. *Philip the evangelist, who was one of the Seven*: Philip was
last heard of on a preaching tour which ended at Caesarea in
8: 40.

evangelist means one who proclaims the good news (Greek,
euangelion).

9. *four unmarried daughters, who possessed the gift of prophecy*:
literally, 'who prophesied', but the N.E.B. doubtless interprets
it correctly.

unmarried: Greek, *parthenoi*, translated in the R.V. 'virgins'.
The same word is used by Paul in the difficult passage on
celibacy in 1 Cor. 7: 25–40. It is possible that these women
had a special ministry in the church.

10. *Agabus*: the man who had prophesied the famine in 11: 28.

11. The premonition of danger at Tyre (verse 4) now becomes a prophecy in the true Old Testament style accompanied by a symbolic action (cf. Jeremiah and his potter's vessel, chapter 19, or his yoke, chapters 27–8)—the reality of the event to come is expressed in the symbol.

12–13. Again Paul refuses to be dissuaded in his purpose.

15–26. Stage 3: To Jerusalem.

16. *Mnason of Cyprus*: one of the early Christians who was to lodge them in Jerusalem.

18–19. Paul at once, *next day*, visited James, who was still the head of the Jerusalem church, and other Christian leaders and reported *in detail* his ministry among the Gentiles.

The last occurrence of the first-person form is in verse 18, having begun in 20: 5 (omitting the address at Miletus in 20: 16–38), until its resumption in 27: 1. This does not mean that the 'we' were not present during the description of the mission which follows. The context assumes that 'we' were.

20–1. Whilst giving *praise to God* for Paul's report the leaders of the Jerusalem church felt it essential that Paul should do something to prove his own zeal for the Law. The Jewish converts in Jerusalem were *staunch upholders of the Law* and worried about rumours that Paul had taught *Jews in the gentile world* (i.e. the Dispersion) to disregard Moses and to cease to circumcise their children. This was obviously not true, as he had even circumcised Timothy who was only technically a Jew (16: 3), but he had to prove his position.

23–4. The four men had probably taken a temporary Nazirite vow (cf. Paul's at Cenchreae, 18: 18) and Paul was asked to pay the expenses of the sacrifices they must offer and *go through the ritual of purification with them*. Paul had not to take the vow himself but the purification would indicate that the rumours about him were false, and that he was *a practising Jew* and kept the Law himself.

25. The repetition of the Council's decisions relating to

gentile converts reaffirms that no change for them is implied. Some manuscripts omit *from anything that has been strangled* as in 15: 20 and 29.

26. Paul fulfilled the requirements of James and his associates but the plan did not succeed. ✻

From Jerusalem to Rome

PAUL IN TROUBLE

27 BUT JUST BEFORE the period of seven days was up, the Jews from the province of Asia saw him in the temple. They stirred up the whole crowd, and seized him,
28 shouting, 'Men of Israel, help, help! This is the fellow who spreads his doctrine all over the world, attacking our people, our law, and this sanctuary. On top of all this he has brought Greeks into the temple and profaned this
29 holy place.' For they had previously seen Trophimus the Ephesian with him in the city, and assumed that Paul had brought him into the temple.

30 The whole city was in a turmoil, and people came running from all directions. They seized Paul and dragged him out of the temple; and at once the doors were shut.
31 While they were clamouring for his death, a report reached the officer commanding the cohort, that all Jeru-
32 salem was in an uproar. He immediately took a force of soldiers with their centurions and came down on the rioters at the double. As soon as they saw the com-
33 mandant and his troops, they stopped beating Paul. The commandant stepped forward, arrested him, and ordered

him to be shackled with two chains; he then asked who
the man was and what he had been doing. Some in the 34
crowd shouted one thing, some another. As he could not
get at the truth because of the hubbub, he ordered him
to be taken into barracks. When Paul reached the steps, 35
he had to be carried by the soldiers because of the violence
of the mob. For the whole crowd were at their heels 36
yelling, 'Kill him!'

Just before Paul was taken into the barracks he said to 37
the commandant, 'May I say something to you?' The
commandant said, 'So you speak Greek, do you? Then 38
you are not the Egyptian who started a revolt some time
ago and led a force of four thousand terrorists out into the
wilds?' Paul replied, 'I am a Jew, a Tarsian from Cilicia, 39
a citizen of no mean city. I ask your permission to speak
to the people.' When permission had been given, Paul 40
stood on the steps and with a gesture called for the attention of the people.

✻ 27–9. In the end it was not the Jerusalem Jews who started
the uproar. As the week for the purification was coming to
an end, some Jews of the Dispersion from Asia *saw him in the
temple*. They accused him of *attacking our people, our law, and
this sanctuary* and above all of bringing Greeks into the Temple.
There was a barrier separating the Court of the Gentiles from
the inner parts of the Temple with warning notices on it
threatening death to Gentiles who passed it. One such inscription was discovered in 1871 in a cemetery, and a portion
of another in 1935 near St Stephen's Gate, in Jerusalem.

The turmoil was engineered on the assumption that Paul
had brought Trophimus the Ephesian (20: 4), who had been
seen with him in the city, into the Temple.

The charges brought against Paul bear a resemblance to

those brought against Stephen, also by Jews of the Dispersion (6: 9–14)—another parallel (see note above on 19: 11–12).

30–6. The description of the tumult is full of action. Once again Luke shows his ability in dramatic representation. The reader is made to feel that he is present.

30. Paul was dragged from the Temple itself into the Court of the Gentiles, which was overlooked by the garrison in the fortress of Antonia, to the north-west of the temple area.

31. *the officer commanding the cohort*: a chiliarch or military tribune in charge of the Jerusalem garrison. A cohort consisted of six centuries, to which some cavalry were attached.

35. *the steps*: from the Court into the barracks.

36. *Kill him!*: literally, 'Away with him', but the N.E.B. captures the exact spirit of the account.

37–40*a*. Paul speaks to the commandant.

38. The commandant must have been surprised when Paul addressed him in Greek, if he thought he was an Egyptian terrorist. The reference may be to a false prophet from Egypt mentioned by Josephus, *Antiquities* xx. 8. 6, who led an attack on the city and was put down by Felix. He may well have assembled his men in *the wilds* before the attack.

terrorists: (R.V. and R.S.V. 'Assassins') Greek, *sicarioi* or 'dagger-men'. Josephus, in the same chapter as he mentions the Egyptian, refers to the *sicarii* or armed robbers in the time of Festus.

39. Paul's reply is a dignified and impressive statement of his credentials. Euripides described Athens in very similar words to those used here by Paul to describe Tarsus. ✶

THE ADDRESS TO THE CROWD

40 As soon as quiet was restored, he addressed them in the Jewish language:

22 'Brothers and fathers, give me a hearing while I make
2 my defence before you.' When they heard him speaking to them in their own language, they listened the more

quietly. 'I am a true-born Jew,' he said, 'a native of ₃
Tarsus in Cilicia. I was brought up in this city, and as a
pupil of Gamaliel I was thoroughly trained in every
point of our ancestral law. I have always been ardent in
God's service, as you all are today. And so I began to ₄
persecute this movement to the death, arresting its followers, men and women alike, and putting them in chains.
For this I have as witnesses the High Priest and the whole ₅
Council of Elders. I was given letters from them to our
fellow-Jews at Damascus, and had started out to bring
the Christians there to Jerusalem as prisoners for punishment; and this is what happened. I was on the road and ₆
nearing Damascus, when suddenly about midday a great
light flashed from the sky all around me, and I fell to the ₇
ground. Then I heard a voice saying to me, "Saul, Saul,
why do you persecute me?" I answered, "Tell me, Lord, ₈
who you are." "I am Jesus of Nazareth," he said, "whom
you are persecuting." My companions saw the light, but ₉
did not hear the voice that spoke to me. "What shall ₁₀
I do, Lord?" I said, and the Lord replied, "Get up and
continue your journey to Damascus; there you will be
told of all the tasks that are laid upon you." As I had been ₁₁
blinded by the brilliance of that light, my companions
led me by the hand, and so I came to Damascus.

'There, a man called Ananias, a devout observer of the ₁₂
Law and well spoken of by all the Jews of that place,
came and stood beside me and said, "Saul, my brother, ₁₃
recover your sight." Instantly I recovered my sight and
saw him. He went on: "The God of our fathers ap- ₁₄
pointed you to know his will and to see the Righteous
One and to hear his very voice, because you are to be his ₁₅

witness before the world, and testify to what you have
16 seen and heard. And now why delay? Be baptized at
once, with invocation of his name, and wash away your
sins."

17 'After my return to Jerusalem, I was praying in the
18 temple when I fell into a trance and saw him there,
speaking to me. "Make haste", he said, "and leave Jerusalem without delay, for they will not accept your testi-
19 mony about me." "Lord," I said, "they know that I
imprisoned those who believe in thee, and flogged them
20 in every synagogue; and when the blood of Stephen thy
witness was shed I stood by, approving, and I looked after
21 the clothes of those who killed him." But he said to me,
"Go, for I am sending you far away to the Gentiles."'

✶ 21: 40*b*. *the Jewish language*: literally, 'the Hebrew
language', i.e. Aramaic. This was tactically a sound move, as
the quietness that followed proved (22: 2).

22: 3. The emphasis throughout the address is on Paul's
Jewish background and witness. He remained all the time a
staunch upholder of the Law.

Gamaliel: the famous Pharisee (5: 34).

as a pupil: a correct interpretation of 'at the feet'.

4. *this movement*: literally, 'the way', as in 9: 2.

5. *Council of Elders*: Sanhedrin.

Luke's emphasis on the story of Paul's conversion has been
noted above, p. 71 . As told in this address the story has the
ring of urgency and purpose. The few slight differences from
the more narrative account in chapter 9 make the events as
told by Paul more realistic and personal.

6. *about midday*: a detail not mentioned in the earlier
account.

8. *of Nazareth*: another additional detail.

9. In this account his companions *saw the light, but did not*

182

hear the voice. In 9: 7, 'they heard the voice but could see no one'.

12–16. Ananias is described here as *a devout observer of the Law and well spoken of by all the Jews of that place.* The emphasis on his orthodoxy is clearly to the point in this address. There is no reference to Ananias' vision nor to Judas' house in Straight Street (9: 10–16). Ananias' words to Paul are extended to emphasize the part played by *the God of our fathers,* who *appointed you to know his will and to see the Righteous One and to hear his very voice.*

14. *the Righteous One*: one of the titles used by Peter for Jesus in 3: 14; it is the equivalent of the Christ, as also in Stephen's speech, 7: 52. Paul's commission was directly from God in the true tradition of Isa. 6: 8 and Jer. 1: 9–10.

16. *with invocation of his name*: literally, 'calling on his name', i.e. accepting Jesus as Lord through baptism and the washing away of sin.

17–21. This vision in the Temple is not mentioned in chapter 9, unless it can be correlated with the events recorded in 9: 26–30; but no reference is made there to a visit to the Temple. Here in Paul's speech it is implied that some time elapsed before he returned from Damascus to Jerusalem so that a vision there would not be very closely connected with his conversion. However, the vision emphasizes that Paul's mission to the Gentiles was directed by God, from his Temple in Jerusalem, after, and only after, rejection by the Jews.

19–20. Not even Paul's proved orthodoxy by his persecution of Stephen and others (7: 58 — 8: 3) would persuade the Jews.

21. The pattern of Paul's future work followed exactly this commission (see at Pisidian Antioch 13: 46–7 and Corinth 18: 6). ✳

THE RESULT

Up to this point they had given him a hearing; but now 22 they began shouting, 'Down with him! A scoundrel like that is better dead!' And as they were yelling and waving 23

24 their cloaks and flinging dust in the air, the commandant
ordered him to be brought into the barracks and gave
instructions to examine him by flogging, and find out
what reason there was for such an outcry against him.
25 But when they tied him up for the lash, Paul said to the
centurion who was standing there, 'Can you legally flog
a man who is a Roman citizen, and moreover has not been
26 found guilty?' When the centurion heard this, he went
and reported it to the commandant. 'What do you
27 mean to do?' he said. 'This man is a Roman citizen.' The
commandant came to Paul. 'Tell me, are you a Roman
28 citizen?' he asked. 'Yes', said he. The commandant rejoined, 'It cost me a large sum to acquire this citizenship.'
29 Paul said, 'But it was mine by birth.' Then those who were
about to examine him withdrew hastily, and the commandant himself was alarmed when he realized that Paul
was a Roman citizen and that he had put him in irons.

* The idea of God sending a mission to the Gentiles was
infuriating and uproar burst out. The dramatic touch is once
more apparent. The commandant cannot believe that Paul
had told him the whole tale (21: 39). There must be more to
confess if the mob was so angry, so he ordered interrogation
by flogging.

23. *waving their cloaks*: literally, 'throwing about their
garments', but the N.E.B. gives the true impression.

25-9. The dignified way in which Paul conducts himself
recalls his release from jail in Philippi (16: 35-40). It is a
remarkably able piece of reporting on Luke's part, throwing
a fascinating light on the characters of both Paul and the
commandant.

25. *for the lash*: a better translation than 'with (the) thongs'
(R.V., R.S.V., and the N.E.B. footnote).

Once again, as a Roman citizen, Paul sought the protection of the law. The Lex Porcia and the Lex Julia forbade the flogging of a Roman citizen (16: 37), and to make the matter worse, Paul pointed out, he had *not been found guilty*.

28–9. *But it was mine by birth*: Paul inherited his citizenship; the commandant's was bought with *a large sum*. The effect of Paul's claim on his examiners was again dramatic. ✳

BEFORE THE SANHEDRIN

The following day, wishing to be quite sure what charge 30 the Jews were bringing against Paul, he released him and ordered the chief priests and the entire Council to assemble. He then took Paul down and stood him before them.

Paul fixed his eyes on the Council and said, 'My **23** brothers, I have lived all my life, and still live today, with a perfectly clear conscience before God.' At this the High 2 Priest Ananias ordered his attendants to strike him on the mouth. Paul retorted, 'God will strike you, you white- 3 washed wall! You sit there to judge me in accordance with the Law; and then in defiance of the Law you order me to be struck!' The attendants said, 'Would you insult 4 God's High Priest?' 'My brothers,' said Paul, 'I had no 5 idea that he was High Priest; Scripture, I know, says: "You must not abuse the ruler of your people."'

Now Paul was well aware that one section of them 6 were Sadducees and the other Pharisees, so he called out in the Council, 'My brothers, I am a Pharisee, a Pharisee born and bred; and the true issue in this trial is our hope of the resurrection of the dead.' At these words the 7 Pharisees and Sadducees fell out among themselves, and the assembly was divided. (The Sadducees deny that there 8

is any resurrection, or angel, or spirit, but the Pharisees
9 accept them.) So a great uproar broke out; and some of
the doctors of the law belonging to the Pharisaic party
openly took sides and declared, 'We can find no fault
with this man; perhaps an angel or spirit has spoken to
10 him.' The dissension was mounting, and the commandant was afraid that Paul would be torn in pieces, so
he ordered the troops to go down, pull him out of the
crowd, and bring him into the barracks.

✻ The affray in the Court of the Gentiles got nowhere and
the commandant was confused. He therefore ordered a
meeting of the Sanhedrin to find out *what charge the Jews were
bringing against Paul*. The account is a summary only of the
proceedings and Luke concentrates solely on Paul's challenge
and the uproar that ensued.

1. Paul's defence is that his conscience is clear. He has not
broken the Law, he has realized its fulfilment in Christianity.

2. Ananias' action demeans the office he held. He was
nominated High Priest in A.D. 48 by Herod Agrippa II and
deposed about ten years later. Josephus, *Antiquities* XX. 9. 2
refers to his evil deeds. He was murdered at the beginning
of the Jewish War.

3. Paul's retort is in keeping with his temperament. Cf.
his anger when Peter came to Antioch (Gal. 2: 11) or when
Barnabas wanted to take Mark on the second expedition
(15: 39).

whitewashed wall: tombs were whitewashed to prevent the
defilement that would follow if anyone should touch them
through not seeing them. It is interesting that Jesus used a
similar phrase in condemning the hypocrisy of the Pharisees
(Matt. 23: 27). Here, Paul uses it to denounce this hypocritical
Sadducee. Luke again introduces a parallel.

5. Paul must have known that Ananias *was* the High Priest.
His reply, therefore, is highly sarcastic. Such a hypocrite

could never be the true High Priest! Paul quotes Exod. 22: 28 to prove he would never have insulted the true *ruler of your people*. For the sake of tranquillity the Roman authorities would still allow the High Priest to be called ruler.

6. Paul makes capital of the disagreement between Pharisees and Sadducees on the doctrine of the resurrection (see note above on 4: 1-22). He, as a Pharisee, raises the question of *our hope of the resurrection of the dead* (literally, 'hope and resurrection', but the N.E.B. gives the meaning). Some commentators suggest *hope* means messianic hope.

8. The parenthesis explains the issue. The Sadducees denied any spiritual world.

9. In their hatred of the Sadducees the Pharisees were prepared to countenance Paul. He might have had a spiritual communication. This was not the first time that the Pharisees had shown appreciation of the Christian point of view (cf. Gamaliel in 5: 35 and the Pharisees who became Christians in 15: 5).

10. Again the uproar was so great that the commandant feared a lynching and sent soldiers to bring Paul back to the barracks. Nothing had been achieved by this move. *

THE PLOT TO KILL PAUL

The following night the Lord appeared to him and said, 11 'Keep up your courage; you have affirmed the truth about me in Jerusalem, and you must do the same in Rome.'

When day broke, the Jews banded together and took an 12 oath not to eat or drink until they had killed Paul. There 13 were more than forty in this conspiracy. They came to 14 the chief priests and elders and said, 'We have bound ourselves by a solemn oath not to taste food until we have killed Paul. It is now for you, acting with the Council, 15 to apply to the commandant to bring him down to you, on the pretext of a closer investigation of his case; and we have arranged to do away with him before he arrives.'

16 But the son of Paul's sister heard of the ambush; he went to the barracks, obtained entry, and reported it to 17 Paul. Paul called one of the centurions and said, 'Take this young man to the commandant; he has something 18 to report.' The centurion took him and brought him to the commandant. 'The prisoner Paul', he said, 'sent for me and asked me to bring this young man to you; he has 19 something to tell you.' The commandant took him by the arm, drew him aside, and asked him, 'What is it you 20 have to report?' He said, 'The Jews have made a plan among themselves and will request you to bring Paul down to the Council tomorrow, on the pretext of ob-21 taining more precise information about him. Do not listen to them; for a party more than forty strong are lying in wait for him. They have sworn not to eat or drink until they have done away with him; they are now 22 ready, and wait only for your consent.' So the commandant dismissed the young man, with orders not to let anyone know that he had given him this information.

✶ 11. Rome was Paul's next objective. The uproar in Jerusalem might well be the means of bringing it about. Paul was very conscious of divine direction (cf. 18: 9–10).

12–22. Again the account is full of drama. It is another episode in the serial play, with still more characters—the forty plotters versus Paul's nephew!

16. A pleasant personal touch. The commandant must have allowed free access to Paul for his family. Perhaps Paul's conversion had separated him from his relatives who now, in his

trouble, became reconciled. Contact again with his family
may also have eased his financial position. He paid the expenses
of the four men under a vow (21: 23–4) and the legal costs
of his trials must have been considerable. Some of Paul's
family must have been members of, or in close contact with,
the Sanhedrin to know of the plot.

20. *on the pretext of obtaining more precise information about
him*: i.e. the Council, as also R.S.V., not the commandant as
R.V. There is manuscript evidence for both. ✶

TO CAESAREA

Then he called a couple of his centurions and issued these 23
orders: 'Get ready two hundred infantry to proceed to
Caesarea, together with seventy cavalrymen and two
hundred light-armed troops; parade three hours after
sunset. Provide also mounts for Paul so that he may ride 24
through under safe escort to Felix the Governor.' And 25
he wrote a letter to this effect:

'Claudius Lysias to His Excellency the Governor Felix. 26
Your Excellency: This man was seized by the Jews and 27
was on the point of being murdered when I intervened
with the troops and removed him, because I discovered
that he was a Roman citizen. As I wished to ascertain the 28
charge on which they were accusing him, I took him
down to their Council. I found that the accusation had 29
to do with controversial matters in their law, but there
was no charge against him meriting death or imprisonment. However, I have now been informed of an attempt 30
to be made on the man's life, so I am sending him to you
at once, and have also instructed his accusers to state their
case against him before you.'

Acting on their orders, the infantry took Paul and 31

32 brought him by night to Antipatris. Next day they returned to their barracks, leaving the cavalry to escort him
33 the rest of the way. The cavalry entered Caesarea, delivered the letter to the Governor, and handed Paul over
34 to him. He read the letter, asked him what province he
35 was from, and learned that he was from Cilicia. 'I will
hear your case', he said, 'when your accusers arrive.' He
then ordered him to be held in custody at his headquarters
in Herod's palace.

✶ This was, in fact, the beginning of the journey to Rome.
The Roman authorities gave Paul, as a Roman citizen, the full
protection of the law. The letter from Claudius Lysias to the
Governor Felix clearly indicated that *there was no charge against
him meriting death or imprisonment* (verse 29). Luke again indicates the friendliness of Rome to the Christians and the determined antagonism of the Jews.

23. It was a very large military escort, but the commandant
was clearly anxious to avoid any more trouble.

light-armed troops: or, as the N.E.B. footnote, 'spearmen',
an unusual Greek word.

three hours after sunset: as a further precaution they were to
set out after dark at 9 p.m.

24. *Felix the Governor*: Felix was procurator of Judaea from
A.D. 52 to 58 or 59 but had been a military prefect in Palestine
before. He was the brother of Pallas, the freedman and
minister of the emperor Claudius. Tacitus had a very poor
opinion of Felix' character. The date of these events is about
A.D. 56-7 (24: 27).

25. *to this effect*: the letter has been composed by Luke but
doubtless contains the main points of what Claudius Lysias
wrote to Felix. It is interesting to have the commandant's
name at last. Hitherto Luke has referred to him by his title.

26. *Excellency*: the title used for Theophilus in Luke 1: 3
and for Festus 26: 25.

27. *because I discovered that he was a Roman citizen*: was not the original reason for intervention but it sums up the reasons for Lysias' present action.

29. *controversial matters in their law*: Gallio had discovered the same (18: 15).

30. The instructions to Paul's accusers had not been mentioned before. Some manuscripts add 'Farewell' to this verse.

31. *Antipatris*: over half-way to Caesarea and thus far enough away from Jerusalem for the escort to be reduced.

34. *learned that he was from Cilicia*: the punctuation in the R.V. and R.S.V. suggests that Felix agreed to hear the case because Paul came from Cilicia, a district under the authority of the legate of Syria, who was Felix' superior, but the N.E.B. implies that it was merely an inquiry regarding his place of origin.

35. *Herod's palace*: Greek, *praetorium*. Once the residence of Herod the Great, now the headquarters of the Roman Governor. ✶

THE TRIAL BEFORE FELIX: I. THE ACCUSATION

Five days later the High Priest Ananias came down, **24** accompanied by some of the elders and an advocate named Tertullus, and they laid an information against Paul before the Governor. When the prisoner was called, 2 Tertullus opened the case.

'Your Excellency,' he said, 'we owe it to you that we enjoy unbroken peace. It is due to your provident care that, in all kinds of ways and in all sorts of places, improvements are being made for the good of this province. We welcome this, sir, most gratefully. And now, not to 3, 4 take up too much of your time, I crave your indulgence for a brief statement of our case. We have found this man 5 to be a perfect pest, a fomenter of discord among the Jews

all over the world, a ringleader of the sect of the Na-
6 zarenes. He even made an attempt to profane the temple;
8 and then we arrested him. If you will examine him yourself you can ascertain from him the truth of all the charges
9 we bring.' The Jews supported the attack, alleging that
the facts were as he stated.

* The gravity of the case, which justified Lysias' considerable
precautions, is clear from the presence of the High Priest
himself at the head of the delegation. Tertullus—another name
in Luke's long list of personalities—was a professional advocate.

2–3. The usual complimentary introduction. Felix did a
great deal to eradicate terrorism.

4. *not to take up too much of your time*: literally, 'not to weary
you'.

5–6. The main charge is that Paul is an anarchist and that
as *a ringleader of the sect of the Nazarenes* he causes trouble *among
the Jews all over the world*. The profanation of the Temple would
not greatly disturb the Governor but it was an example of the
trouble Paul caused.

(7) Some manuscripts add: 'It was our intention to try him
under our law; but Lysias the commandant intervened and
took him by force out of our hands, (8) ordering his accusers
to come before you.' This criticism of Lysias would not help
their cause before the Governor. The addition is probably due
to a desire to conform the narrative to the earlier account and
so clarify what would otherwise appear to be an incoherent
statement. *

THE TRIAL BEFORE FELIX: II. THE DEFENCE

10 Then the Governor motioned to Paul to speak, and he
began his reply: 'Knowing as I do that for many years
you have administered justice in this province, I make my
11 defence with confidence. You can ascertain the facts for

yourself. It is not more than twelve days since I went up
to Jerusalem on a pilgrimage. They did not find me 12
arguing with anyone, or collecting a crowd, either in the
temple or in the synagogues or up and down the city;
and they cannot make good the charges they bring against 13
me. But this much I will admit: I am a follower of the 14
new way (the "sect" they speak of), and it is in that
manner that I worship the God of our fathers; for I believe
all that is written in the Law and the prophets, and in 15
reliance on God I hold the hope, which my accusers too
accept, that there is to be a resurrection of good and wicked
alike. Accordingly I, no less than they, train myself to 16
keep at all times a clear conscience before God and man.

'After an absence of several years I came to bring 17
charitable gifts to my nation and to offer sacrifices. They 18
found me in the temple ritually purified and engaged in
this service. I had no crowd with me, and there was no
disturbance. But some Jews from the province of Asia
were there, and if they had any charge against me it is 19
they who ought to have been in court to state it. Failing 20
that, it is for these persons here present to say what crime
they discovered when I was brought before the Council,
apart from this one open assertion which I made as I stood 21
there: "The true issue in my trial before you today is the
resurrection of the dead."'

✻ Like Tertullus, Paul begins with the usual complimentary
address, and then he summarizes the events of the last twelve
days. He denies the charges of causing a disturbance, saying
that he had gone to Jerusalem *on a pilgrimage* (the verb means
'to worship').

14. *the new way*: literally, 'the way', i.e. the Christian way

(see above 9: 2; 18: 26), by which he claimed to *worship the God of our fathers* as a true Jew; *for I believe all that is written in the Law and the prophets.*

(*the 'sect' they speak of*): R.V. margin, 'heresy'. The Greek word is *haeresis* from which 'heresy' comes.

15. *the hope...that there is to be a resurrection* would be held only by the Pharisees. Perhaps Paul was again working upon the differences in teaching among his accusers (see on 23: 6).

of good and wicked alike: according to Dan. 12: 2, 'many of them that sleep in the dust of the earth shall awake, some to everlasting life, and some to shame and everlasting contempt'.

17. The purpose of his return to Jerusalem was *to bring charitable gifts to my nation*, and of his presence in the Temple *to offer sacrifices*. It is a curious fact that this sentence alone in Acts seems to refer to Paul's collection from the gentile churches for the poor in Jerusalem, on which he lays much stress in his letters (Rom. 15: 25–8; 1 Cor. 16: 1–3; 2 Cor. 8: 1–4; 9: 1–2). So far it had not been relevant to Luke's story (see note on 20: 3) but it is clearly of importance in his defence. Far from causing trouble he had come with financial help to his countrymen.

17–18 a. The offering of sacrifices and the ritual purification in the Temple, which he had carried out with the 'four men ...who are under a vow' (21: 23) showed his loyalty to Jewish tradition.

18 b–19. It was while he was performing this religious act that *some Jews from the province of Asia* found him, but they were not in court to bring any charge.

20–1. So far as those members of the Sanhedrin who were present were concerned, they knew that no crime had been found in Paul when he was examined before their full Council, except that he had said: '*The true issue in my trial before you today is the resurrection of the dead*' (cf. 23: 6). Such an issue was, of course, purely one of Jewish doctrine, and of which a Roman court would take no cognizance. ✻

THE TRIAL BEFORE FELIX: III. THE ADJOURNMENT

Then Felix, who happened to be well informed about the 22
Christian movement, adjourned the hearing. 'When
Lysias the commanding officer comes down', he said,
'I will go into your case.' He gave orders to the centurion 23
to keep Paul under open arrest and not to prevent any of
his friends from making themselves useful to him.

Some days later Felix came with his wife Drusilla, who 24
was a Jewess, and sending for Paul he let him talk to him
about faith in Christ Jesus. But when the discourse turned 25
to questions of morals, self-control, and the coming judgement, Felix became alarmed and exclaimed, 'That will
do for the present; when I find it convenient I will send
for you again.' At the same time he had hopes of a bribe 26
from Paul; and for this reason he sent for him very often
and talked with him. When two years had passed, Felix 27
was succeeded by Porcius Festus. Wishing to curry favour
with the Jews, Felix left Paul in custody.

✻ 22–3. As Felix *happened to be well informed about the Christian
movement* (literally, 'the way'), presumably to its advantage, he
adjourned the hearing until Lysias should come. We never hear
that he did come and meanwhile Paul was kept in free custody
so that his friends could visit him. Felix clearly regarded him
as innocent.

24–7. This private discussion with the Governor, one of
many (verse 26), enables Luke to introduce Drusilla, who, as
a Jewess, was probably interested in Christianity. She was the
daughter of Herod Agrippa I (12: 1) and sister of Herod
Agrippa II and Bernice (25: 13). She had married King Aziz
of Emesa (see map, p. 17) but Felix had recently seduced her
from him. Paul's discourse on *morals, self-control, and the*

coming judgement might well alarm Felix! (See p. x for the Herod family.)

26. *hopes of a bribe*: presumably Paul or his friends had money at this time (see note on 23: 16).

27. To avoid further trouble with the Jews Felix kept Paul *in custody* for the remaining two years of his procuratorship, and then Porcius Festus succeeded him. ✳

FESTUS TAKES UP THE CASE

25 Three days after taking up his appointment Festus went
2 up from Caesarea to Jerusalem, where the chief priests and the Jewish leaders brought before him the case against
3 Paul. They asked Festus to favour them against him, and pressed for him to be brought up to Jerusalem, for they
4 were planning an ambush to kill him on the way. Festus, however, replied, 'Paul is in safe custody at Caesarea, and
5 I shall be leaving Jerusalem shortly myself; so let your leading men come down with me, and if there is anything wrong, let them prosecute him.'

6   After spending eight or ten days at most in Jerusalem, he went down to Caesarea, and next day he took his seat
7 in court and ordered Paul to be brought up. When he appeared, the Jews who had come down from Jerusalem stood round bringing many grave charges, which they
8 were unable to prove. Paul's plea was: 'I have committed no offence, either against the Jewish law, or
9 against the temple, or against the Emperor.' Festus, anxious to ingratiate himself with the Jews, turned to Paul and asked, 'Are you willing to go up to Jerusalem and
10 stand trial on these charges before me there?' But Paul said, 'I am now standing before the Emperor's tribunal,

and that is where I must be tried. Against the Jews I have
committed no offence, as you very well know. If I am   11
guilty of any capital crime, I do not ask to escape the
death penalty; but if there is no substance in the charges
which these men bring against me, it is not open to anyone to hand me over as a sop to them. I appeal to Caesar!'
Then Festus, after conferring with his advisers, replied,   12
'You have appealed to Caesar: to Caesar you shall go.'

☆ Despite the length of time that Paul was 'left in custody'
at Caesarea, the Jews in Jerusalem had not forgotten him. As
soon as the new procurator, Porcius Festus, arrived on his first
official visit to the city *the Jewish leaders brought before him the
case against Paul.* They hoped to have him brought to Jerusalem and had revived the plot *to kill him on the way* (see
23: 12).

1. *Festus*: Porcius Festus was procurator from A.D. 58 or 59
to 61 or 62. He died in office.

4–5. Festus clearly intends to be firm with the Jews but
invites their leaders to come to Caesarea.

6. Festus realizes that Paul's case is very important for
Jewish–Roman relations and tries it immediately on his return.

7–8. Luke dismisses the *many grave charges, which they were
unable to prove* in a short sentence, and sums up Paul's defence
that he had *committed no offence* against the *law,…the temple,
or…the Emperor* equally briefly.

9. The procurator is anxious to conciliate the Jews and asks
Paul if he will be tried in his own court in Jerusalem.

10–11. A dignified comment in line with Paul's other statements when his citizenship is involved (at Philippi, 16: 37–8;
at Jerusalem, 22: 25–9). He is now before *the Emperor's*
provincial *tribunal* and, as justice does not seem possible there,
he appeals, as a Roman citizen, to be tried in Rome itself.

12. Festus, *after conferring with his* legal *advisers,* allowed the
appeal. ☆

THE STATE VISIT OF HEROD AGRIPPA II
AND BERNICE

13 After an interval of some days King Agrippa and Bernice
14 arrived at Caesarea on a courtesy visit to Festus. They
spent several days there, and during this time Festus laid
Paul's case before the king. 'We have a man', he said,
15 'left in custody by Felix; and when I was in Jerusalem
the chief priests and elders of the Jews laid an information
16 against him, demanding his condemnation. I answered
them, "It is not Roman practice to hand over any accused
man before he is confronted with his accusers and given
17 an opportunity of answering the charge." So when they
had come here with me I lost no time; the very next day
I took my seat in court and ordered the man to be brought
18 up. But when his accusers rose to speak, they brought
19 none of the charges I was expecting; they merely had
certain points of disagreement with him about their peculiar religion, and about someone called Jesus, a dead
20 man whom Paul alleged to be alive. Finding myself out
of my depth in such discussions, I asked if he was willing
to go to Jerusalem and stand his trial there on these issues.
21 But Paul appealed to be remanded in custody for His
Imperial Majesty's decision, and I ordered him to be de-
22 tained until I could send him to the Emperor.' Agrippa
said to Festus, 'I should rather like to hear the man myself.'
'Tomorrow', he answered, 'you shall hear him.'

23 So next day Agrippa and Bernice came in full state and
entered the audience-chamber accompanied by high-
ranking officers and prominent citizens; and on the orders
24 of Festus Paul was brought up. Then Festus said, 'King

Agrippa, and all you gentlemen here present with us, you see this man: the whole body of the Jews approached me both in Jerusalem and here, loudly insisting that he had no right to remain alive. But it was clear to me that he 25 had committed no capital crime, and when he himself appealed to His Imperial Majesty, I decided to send him. But I have nothing definite about him to put in writing 26 for our Sovereign. Accordingly I have brought him up before you all and particularly before you, King Agrippa, so that as a result of this preliminary inquiry I may have something to report. There is no sense, it seems to me, 27 in sending on a prisoner without indicating the charges against him.'

✻ In a sense, the considerable section 25: 13 — 26: 32 does not advance the narrative at all. Paul had appealed to Caesar and to Caesar he had to go. The colourful state visit of Agrippa and Bernice, however, enabled Luke to obtain a considered opinion from an influential and well-informed *Jew* that 'The fellow could have been discharged, if he had not appealed to the Emperor' (26: 32). In addition Luke, as usual, enjoyed writing another striking scene for his drama, peopled by Agrippa and his court; and, in Paul's defence before the king, he was given the opportunity for the third time to describe Paul's conversion—that event so indicative of the work of the Spirit and so vital for the growth of the church.

13. *King Agrippa and Bernice*: Agrippa II, son of Herod Agrippa I (12: 1), who died in A.D. 44 (see family tree, p. x). Agrippa II had been made King of Chalcis in the Lebanon and to this territory had been added the tetrarchies of Philip and Lysanias and some cities in Galilee and Peraea. He had the right of nominating the High Priest and had recently deposed Ananias. It is worth noting that Paul's case continued despite this change in the High Priesthood. Bernice

was the sister of Agrippa II and also of Drusilla, Felix' wife (24: 24).

15–22. Luke must have had close contact with the procurator's household to get so detailed a report of this conversation, or else he is simply writing a coherent account, largely deduced from the public hearing (verses 23 ff.), for which he might well have more direct evidence.

16. Another expression of approval of Roman legal practice.

18–19. Like Gallio (18: 14–15), Festus had little interest in or understanding of *their peculiar religion* and especially the *someone called Jesus, a dead man whom Paul alleged to be alive.*

20. This sounds as if Festus referred to the Sanhedrin, but verse 9 makes it clear he meant the procurator's court. The reason given in verse 9 for Festus' offer of a Jerusalem trial is less complimentary to him than the one here.

21. *His Imperial Majesty*: (see also verse 25) Greek, *Sebastos*, i.e. Augustus; the R.V. and R.S.V. translate 'emperor', retaining 'Caesar' for the N.E.B. *Emperor* at the end of the verse.

23. A pictorial description of the *audience-chamber.*

26. Festus hoped from Agrippa's hearing of Paul's defence to obtain something *definite about him to put in writing for our Sovereign* (Greek, *kyrios*, 'lord', an early use of the word for 'emperor'). ✶

BEFORE AGRIPPA

26 Agrippa said to Paul, 'You have our permission to speak for yourself.' Then Paul stretched out his hand and began his defence:

2   'I consider myself fortunate, King Agrippa, that it is before you that I am to make my defence today upon all
3 the charges brought against me by the Jews, particularly as you are expert in all Jewish matters, both our customs and our disputes. And therefore I beg you to give me a patient hearing.

'My life from my youth up, the life I led from the 4
beginning among my people and in Jerusalem, is familiar
to all Jews. Indeed they have known me long enough 5
and could testify, if they only would, that I belonged to
the strictest group in our religion: I lived as a Pharisee.
And it is for a hope kindled by God's promise to our 6
forefathers that I stand in the dock today. Our twelve 7
tribes hope to see the fulfilment of that promise, worshipping with intense devotion day and night; and for
this very hope I am impeached, and impeached by Jews,
Your Majesty. Why is it considered incredible among 8
you that God should raise dead men to life?

'I myself once thought it my duty to work actively 9
against the name of Jesus of Nazareth; and I did so in 10
Jerusalem. It was I who imprisoned many of God's
people by authority obtained from the chief priests; and
when they were condemned to death, my vote was cast
against them. In all the synagogues I tried by repeated 11
punishment to make them renounce their faith; indeed
my fury rose to such a pitch that I extended my persecution to foreign cities.

'On one such occasion I was travelling to Damascus 12
with authority and commission from the chief priests;
and as I was on my way, Your Majesty, in the middle of 13
the day I saw a light from the sky, more brilliant than the
sun, shining all around me and my travelling-companions.
We all fell to the ground, and then I heard a voice saying 14
to me in the Jewish language, "Saul, Saul, why do you
persecute me? It is hard for you, this kicking against the
goad." I said, "Tell me, Lord, who you are"; and the 15
Lord replied, "I am Jesus, whom you are persecuting.

16 But now, rise to your feet and stand upright. I have appeared to you for a purpose: to appoint you my servant and witness, to testify both to what you have seen and to
17 what you shall yet see of me. I will rescue you from this people and from the Gentiles to whom I am sending
18 you. I send you to open their eyes and turn them from darkness to light, from the dominion of Satan to God, so that, by trust in me, they may obtain forgiveness of sins, and a place with those whom God has made his own."

19   'And so, King Agrippa, I did not disobey the heavenly
20 vision. I turned first to the inhabitants of Damascus, and then to Jerusalem and all the country of Judaea, and to the Gentiles, and sounded the call to repent and turn to
21 God, and to prove their repentance by deeds. That is why the Jews seized me in the temple and tried to do away
22 with me. But I had God's help, and so to this very day I stand and testify to great and small alike. I assert nothing beyond what was foretold by the prophets and by Moses:
23 that the Messiah must suffer, and that he, the first to rise from the dead, would announce the dawn to Israel and to the Gentiles.'

✻ Paul's defence is geared to his well-informed, educated audience. It bears the impress of a natural orator but is sufficiently personal to avoid any danger of becoming stilted.

1–3. After an introductory gesture, Paul made the usual complimentary address (cf. Tertullus and Paul before Felix, 24: 2 and 10). Agrippa is the ideal judge because of his own expert knowledge of Jewish *customs* and *disputes*.

4–5. Paul's upbringing and training as a Pharisee were so well known that he does not repeat the details this time (cf. the speech from the steps of the fort, 22: 3).

6. As a devout Jew his hope was for the coming of the Messiah, and as a Pharisee this was linked with resurrection.

7. Towards this hope the whole of Israel's worship, *day and night*, was directed and yet it was Jews who had *impeached* him.

Your Majesty: literally, 'O king', cf. verse 13.

8. The rhetorical question had been answered already. The hope of a Messiah included his resurrection.

9–11. There was a time when Paul himself had persecuted those who believed in *the name of Jesus of Nazareth*. The brief references made to Paul's attack on the church in 8: 3, 9: 1 and 22: 4 are extended here to impress upon his hearers his own part in the persecution. In an argument, no man can speak with such authority as the one who has personal knowledge of both sides. His evidence is the most convincing.

12–18. For the third time the details of Paul's conversion are recounted by Luke. Again there are slight differences which make it more applicable to his present audience. This time the brightness of the light is emphasized by describing it as *more brilliant than the sun, shining all around me and my travelling-companions*. At this divine revelation, *all* (not Paul only as in 9: 4 and 22: 7) *fell to the ground*. The voice is said explicitly to have spoken *in the Jewish language* (literally, 'Hebrew', i.e. Aramaic, the language Jesus used). In the other accounts its use is implied by the use of the Aramaic name 'Saul' in the address.

14. '*It is hard for you, this kicking against the goad*': another addition to the earlier accounts. It is a Greek proverb, not known in Aramaic.

15–18. The commission is direct from Jesus. There is no question of the human intervention of Ananias, who does not appear. It is a divine command. '*I have appeared to you for a purpose: to appoint you my servant and witness, to testify both to what you have seen and to what you shall yet see of me.*' It is no wonder that Paul included himself as an apostle, though inferior to all the others and 'indeed not fit to be called an apostle' (1 Cor. 15: 9).

17. Paul's work is to be amongst Jews and Gentiles, though from both he will need divine protection. The substance of this had been proved repeatedly on his journeys.

18. There is no overt reference in this account to Paul's blindness at his conversion, but the quotation from Isa. 42: 7 and 16 may imply a hidden application of it to those with whom he is to work. He himself had passed '*from darkness to light, from the dominion of Satan to God.*' Who, then, was better equipped to lead others? He had received the reward of '*forgiveness of sins, and a place with those whom God has made his own.*' So will they.

19-23. As a result of the vision Paul *sounded the call to repent and turn to God*, first in *Damascus*, then *Jerusalem*, then *Judaea* and finally to *the Gentiles*. Surely no Jew could object to such work and yet this is why they tried to murder him, *in the temple* of all places! God stood by him, however, and so he was saved for further work.

22 b-3. This is a summary of the whole Christian message:

(i) It is based only on *what was foretold by the prophets and by Moses* (cf. the similar teaching in Paul's defence before Felix, 24: 14-15), namely,

(ii) *that the Messiah must suffer, and*

(iii) *that he, the first to rise from the dead, would announce the dawn to Israel and to the Gentiles* (literally, 'light both to the people and to the nations'). Thus the prophecy of Simeon (Luke 2: 32) would be fulfilled. Jesus was the Messiah; he had suffered; he had risen from the dead; and he had brought the light of salvation to Israel and to the Gentiles. ✳

THE RESULT

24 While Paul was thus making his defence, Festus shouted at the top of his voice, 'Paul, you are raving; too much
25 study is driving you mad.' 'I am not mad, Your Ex-
26 cellency,' said Paul; 'what I am saying is sober truth. The king is well versed in these matters, and to him I can

speak freely. I do not believe that he can be unaware of
any of these facts, for this has been no hole-and-corner
business. King Agrippa, do you believe the prophets? 27
I know you do.' Agrippa said to Paul, 'You think 28
it will not take much to win me over and make a
Christian of me.' 'Much or little,' said Paul, 'I wish to 29
God that not only you, but all those also who are listening to me today, might become what I am, apart from
these chains.'

With that the king rose, and with him the Governor, 30
Bernice, and the rest of the company, and after they had 31
withdrawn they talked it over. 'This man', they said,
'is doing nothing that deserves death or imprisonment.'
Agrippa said to Festus, 'The fellow could have been dis- 32
charged, if he had not appealed to the Emperor.'

✳ 24. Festus' interruption makes the conclusion of Paul's
speech even more impressive than if it had been properly
rounded off. The whole appeal is beyond the procurator. He
can only think Paul is mad.

25-6. Paul's reaction to Festus' outburst is calmly dignified.
King Agrippa, as an educated Jew, will certainly know the
facts. *This has been no hole-and-corner business* (literally, 'done
in a corner', a Greek proverb).

27. Agrippa knew what the prophets foretold. It was an
essential part of Jewish faith.

28. A difficult sentence. The N.E.B. gives the right interpretation. Agrippa's reply is neither a sarcastic rejoinder nor
the heartfelt cry of a man on the threshold of conviction. It is
the winsome reaction of a thoughtful man who sees the point
but will not be convinced. The Greek is very concise: 'In a
short time' (or 'with little effort') 'you persuade me to make
a Christian' (or 'to turn Christian').

29. Paul's reply is almost a prayer. With the same calm

dignity he longs for them all to become as he is, *apart from these chains*.

30–2. The whole company agreed that *This man is doing nothing that deserves death or imprisonment*. Doubtless the procurator's report to the Emperor would bear this in mind. *If he had not appealed to the Emperor*, there would have been nothing to hinder his discharge. ✻

TO ROME

✻ From Caesarea to Rome is one long 'we-section', full of the thrill of an exciting and dangerous sea-voyage. Not only is the story made more thrilling by the personal comments of Luke as an eyewitness, but it gives a vivid impression of Paul as a person. Although this breathless narrative has been divided for ease of comment, it ought first to be read without a pause from 27: 1 to 28: 15. ✻

STAGE I: TO CRETE

27 When it was decided that we should sail for Italy, Paul and some other prisoners were handed over to a cen-
2 turion named Julius, of the Augustan Cohort. We embarked in a ship of Adramyttium, bound for ports in the province of Asia, and put out to sea. In our party was
3 Aristarchus, a Macedonian from Thessalonica. Next day we landed at Sidon; and Julius very considerately allowed
4 Paul to go to his friends to be cared for. Leaving Sidon we sailed under the lee of Cyprus because of the head-
5 winds, then across the open sea off the coast of Cilicia and Pamphylia, and so reached Myra in Lycia.

6 There the centurion found an Alexandrian vessel bound
7 for Italy and put us aboard. For a good many days we made little headway, and we were hard put to it to reach

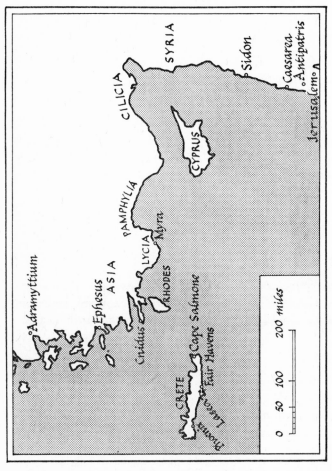

The voyage from Caesarea to Crete

Cnidus. Then, as the wind continued against us, off Sal-
8 mone we began to sail under the lee of Crete, and, hugging the coast, struggled on to a place called Fair Havens,
not far from the town of Lasea.

9 By now much time had been lost, the Fast was already
over, and it was risky to go on with the voyage. Paul
10 therefore gave them this advice: 'I can see, gentlemen,'
he said, 'that this voyage will be disastrous: it will mean
grave loss, loss not only of ship and cargo but also of life.'
11 But the centurion paid more attention to the captain and
12 to the owner of the ship than to what Paul said; and as
the harbour was unsuitable for wintering, the majority
were in favour of putting out to sea, hoping, if they could
get so far, to winter at Phoenix, a Cretan harbour exposed
south-west and north-west.

✻ 1. *Augustan Cohort*: presumably the Cohors Augusta I
which was in Syria during the first century A.D. W. M. Ramsay
(*St Paul the Traveller and the Roman Citizen*, p. 315) suggested
that it was a 'corps of officer-couriers', known as *frumentarii*,
in the immediate service of the Emperor and to whom a task
like the one committed to *Julius* might well have been assigned.

2. *a ship of Adramyttium*: a coaster, whose home port was
Adramyttium, near Assos and Troas.

Aristarchus: already mentioned twice in Acts, at Ephesus
(19: 29) and in Macedonia (20: 4), a close companion of Paul
(Col. 4: 10 and Philem. 24).

3. Julius clearly regarded Paul as in a different category
from his other prisoners, hence he allowed him ashore at
Sidon to visit his friends (probably members of the church
there).

4–5. *under the lee of Cyprus*, i.e. between the island and the
mainland, *because of the head-winds*: the prevailing winds in
the late summer (see verse 9) are westerly, and hence the sailors

took advantage of the island first and then of *the coast of Cilicia and Pamphylia* until they *reached Myra in Lycia*.

6. The ship of Adramyttium would now proceed north so Julius transferred his party to *an Alexandrian vessel* taking grain to Italy (see verse 38 where the cargo is jettisoned).

7-8. The voyage west to *Cnidus*, the most south-western point on the mainland, was slow and difficult. The weather was threatening, so they sailed south, rounded Cape *Salmone*, the eastern promontory of Crete, and, *hugging the coast, struggled on to...Fair Havens*, a bay near *Lasea* on the south coast.

9. The voyage had been so slow that the autumn gales would soon be upon them. *The Fast*, i.e. the Day of Atonement, which usually falls early in October, had passed, which meant that *it was risky to go on with the voyage*. According to Vegetius, *De Re Militari*, the period from mid-September to 11 November was dangerous for sailing on the open sea, and, after that, navigation ceased for the winter.

10-11. Paul's warning is simply that of an experienced traveller. Although his advice was disregarded in favour of that of the professionals, he was obviously listened to.

11-12. Fair Havens was an open bay, of use only for temporary shelter, therefore *the captain* and *the owner of the ship* advised trying to reach *Phoenix, a Cretan harbour exposed south-west and north-west* (the Greek words are the names of the south-west and north-west winds and so presumably refer to the breakwaters of the harbour). ✻

STAGE II: TO MALTA

So when a southerly breeze sprang up, they thought that 13 their purpose was as good as achieved, and, weighing anchor, they sailed along the coast of Crete hugging the land. But before very long a fierce wind, the 'North- 14 easter' as they call it, tore down from the landward side.

15 It caught the ship and, as it was impossible to keep head
16 to wind, we had to give way and run before it. We ran
under the lee of a small island called Cauda, and with a
struggle managed to get the ship's boat under control.
17 When they had hoisted it aboard, they made use of tackle
and undergirded the ship. Then, because they were afraid
of running on to the shallows of Syrtis, they lowered the

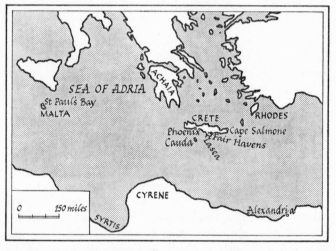

The voyage from Crete to Malta

18 mainsail and let her drive. Next day, as we were making
19 very heavy weather, they began to lighten the ship; and
on the third day they jettisoned the ship's gear with their
20 own hands. For days on end there was no sign of either
sun or stars, a great storm was raging, and our last hopes
of coming through alive began to fade.
21 When they had gone for a long time without food,
Paul stood up among them and said, 'You should have

taken my advice, gentlemen, not to sail from Crete; then
you would have avoided this damage and loss. But now 22
I urge you not to lose heart; not a single life will be lost,
only the ship. For last night there stood by me an angel 23
of the God whose I am and whom I worship. "Do not be 24
afraid, Paul," he said; "it is ordained that you shall appear
before the Emperor; and, be assured, God has granted you
the lives of all who are sailing with you." So keep up your 25
courage: I trust in God that it will turn out as I have been
told; though we have to be cast ashore on some island.' 26

✻ 13. The *southerly breeze* deceived them into making an
attempt to reach Phoenix.

14. *a fierce wind, the 'North-easter' as they call it* (Greek,
Euraquilo, a stormy wind from the mountains of Crete),
drove them out to sea.

16. The protection of the *small island called Cauda* (or Clauda
in some manuscripts) enabled them to take the ship's dinghy
on board.

17. *they made use of tackle and undergirded the ship*: the tech-
nical details of the way in which the ship was prepared for
running before the storm are not clear to us now, but the
pattern of events can readily be followed. After the rowing-
boat had been *hoisted...aboard*, an attempt would be made to
prevent the seams of the ship from springing leaks. In a violent
storm the quickest way of accomplishing this would be to
lower weighted ropes on the leeward side of the ship for her
to drift over, and then for them to be hauled up on the other
side and made fast, thus binding the ship's timbers together
to withstand the strain.

the shallows of Syrtis: at present the wind was driving them
south-westwards towards the sandbanks, known as the Syrtis,
on the North African coast.

they lowered the mainsail: the Greek means 'they let loose
the gear or tackling'. The N.E.B. is probably right if it means

that they were trying to keep the head of the ship up into the wind, but suggestions have also been made that it means they lowered an anchor or weighted rope from the stern to check the ship's speed.

18–19. There was a danger of the ship settling, so all the deck gear was thrown overboard *to lighten* it.

gear: the feminine version of the neuter noun in verse 17.

20. The storm prevented them from checking their position by *sun or stars* and *hopes of coming through alive began to fade.*

21–6. This passage throws a most interesting light on Paul's character. With only a brief reference to his earlier warning (verse 10), he stands out as the one strong man in a terrified and hungry ship-load. His confidence in the divine revelation gives his companions renewed hope and encouragement. He knew that he must *appear before the Emperor* and he trusted *in God* that, although they would be shipwrecked *on some island*, there would be no loss of life. The guidance of the Holy Spirit during the voyage to Rome is comparable with that during Paul's stay in Corinth (18: 9–10) and follows the prophecy in Jerusalem (23: 11). ✲

STAGE III: THE WRECK

27 The fourteenth night came and we were still drifting in
the Sea of Adria. In the middle of the night the sailors
28 felt that land was getting nearer. They sounded and found
twenty fathoms. Sounding again after a short interval
29 they found fifteen fathoms; and fearing that we might be
cast ashore on a rugged coast they dropped four anchors
30 from the stern and prayed for daylight to come. The
sailors tried to abandon ship; they had already lowered
the ship's boat, pretending they were going to lay out
31 anchors from the bows, when Paul said to the centurion
and the soldiers, 'Unless these men stay on board you can

none of you come off safely.' So the soldiers cut the ropes 32
of the boat and let her drop away.

Shortly before daybreak Paul urged them all to take 33
some food. 'For the last fourteen days', he said, 'you
have lived in suspense and gone hungry; you have eaten
nothing whatever. So I beg you to have something to 34
eat; your lives depend on it. Remember, not a hair of
your heads will be lost.' With these words, he took 35
bread, gave thanks to God in front of them all, broke it,
and began eating. Then they all plucked up courage, and 36
took food themselves. There were on board two hundred 37
and seventy-six of us in all. When they had eaten as much 38
as they wanted they lightened the ship by dumping the
corn in the sea.

When day broke they could not recognize the land, 39
but they noticed a bay with a sandy beach, on which they
planned, if possible, to run the ship ashore. So they slipped 40
the anchors and let them go; at the same time they
loosened the lashings of the steering-paddles, set the foresail to the wind, and let her drive to the beach. But they 41
found themselves caught between cross-currents and ran
the ship aground, so that the bow stuck fast and remained
immovable, while the stern was being pounded to pieces
by the breakers. The soldiers thought they had better kill 42
the prisoners for fear that any should swim away and
escape; but the centurion wanted to bring Paul safely 43
through and prevented them from carrying out their
plan. He gave orders that those who could swim should
jump overboard first and get to land; the rest were to 44
follow, some on planks, some on parts of the ship. And
thus it was that all came safely to land.

✻ Luke takes full advantage of the situation to tell the story as dramatically as possible.

27. *Sea of Adria*: i.e. that part of the Mediterranean south of the present Adriatic. After a fortnight's drifting, during the night *the sailors felt that land was getting nearer*. Perhaps they heard breakers.

28–9. When they found the soundings reduced to fifteen fathoms, *they dropped four anchors from the stern*.

30–2. The attempt of the crew to reach the shore, despite the darkness, before the ship broke up is understandable. Their morale was very low, as is clear from what Paul said to them (verse 33), and they were distraught. Paul realized what they were about. Anchors from the bows would achieve nothing with the gale blowing from the stern. The only hope was for the sailors to remain on board and use their skill in running the ship ashore as soon as day broke. *So the soldiers cut the ropes of the boat*, which had been lowered, *and let her drop away*.

33–6. Again Paul stands out prominently as a man of courage and commonsense. They must eat to be ready for the task of beaching the ship. He therefore publicly—*in front of them all*—said grace *and began eating. Then they all plucked up courage, and took food themselves*. They were probably encouraged by Paul's reminder of God's promise (verse 24) that they should all be saved. The meal is clearly not a Communion, though the words in verse 35 are reminiscent of those in Luke 22: 19.

37. *Two hundred and seventy-six* sounds a rather large number. Some manuscripts read 'about seventy-six'.

38. The *dumping the corn in the sea* was to lighten the ship as much as possible for the beaching operations.

39–41. The beach where they planned *to run the ship ashore* corresponds fairly accurately with St Paul's Bay at the north-west corner of the island of Malta. The ship was well placed for the beaching. The anchors to the stern were cut away; *the steering-paddles*, which had been lashed in the storm, were left loose; the small foresail was hoisted *to the wind*; and the ship drove ashore. She struck on a mudbank *between cross-currents* (Greek, 'between two seas'). *The bow stuck fast* while the stern was *pounded to pieces by the breakers.*

42-3 a. The soldiers feared their prisoners would escape and wanted to kill them, but the centurion, in his concern for Paul, *prevented them from carrying out their plan.* No doubt the centurion was well aware of the importance of bringing Paul, the Roman citizen, to Rome and was also probably grateful to him for his support during the voyage.

43 b-4. The centurion then ordered the swimmers to *jump overboard first and get to land*; and then the rest were to make for the shore on wreckage from the ship. *And thus it was that all came safely to land.* *

STAGE IV: IN MALTA

Once we had made our way to safety we identified the **28** island as Malta. The rough islanders treated us with un- 2 common kindness: because it was cold and had started to rain, they lit a bonfire and made us all welcome. Paul 3 had got together an armful of sticks and put them on the fire, when a viper, driven out by the heat, fastened on his hand. The islanders, seeing the snake hanging on to his 4 hand, said to one another, 'The man must be a murderer; he may have escaped from the sea, but divine justice has not let him live.' Paul, however, shook off the snake into 5 the fire and was none the worse. They still expected that 6 any moment he would swell up or drop down dead, but after waiting a long time without seeing anything extra-ordinary happen to him, they changed their minds and now said, 'He is a god.'

In the neighbourhood of that place there were lands belonging to the chief magistrate of the island, whose

name was Publius. He took us in and entertained us hos-
8 pitably for three days. It so happened that this man's
father was in bed suffering from recurrent bouts of fever
and dysentery. Paul visited him and, after prayer, laid his
9 hands upon him and healed him; whereupon the other
10 sick people on the island came also and were cured. They
honoured us with many marks of respect, and when we
were leaving they put on board provision for our needs.

✶ 1. The island was soon *identified...as Malta* (Greek, *Melite*
or *Melitene*, but clearly the island now known as Malta).

2. *The rough islanders* (Greek, 'barbarians', i.e. 'non-Greeks')
welcomed the shipwrecked *with uncommon kindness*. The
N.E.B. seems to stress the primitive nature of the islanders,
apparently from their reaction to the snake which attacked
Paul, but the word 'barbarians' need not have this implication.

3–6. When Paul was gathering sticks for the fire *a viper,
driven out by the heat* bit him. The natives thereupon said, *The
man must be a murderer; he may have escaped from the sea, but
divine justice* (Greek, *dike*, 'justice' or 'right') *has not let him live*;
but when Paul shook the snake into the fire and took no harm,
they said, *He is a god*. Luke thus believed that Jesus' words
had proved true: 'I have given you the power to tread under-
foot snakes and scorpions...and nothing will ever harm you'
(Luke 10: 19).

7–10. The work of the Spirit was manifested further in the
healing of Publius' father from *bouts of fever and dysentery* and
of *other sick people on the island*.

the chief magistrate of the island, whose name was Publius:
literally, 'the first man of the island'. The N.E.B. correctly
interprets it as an official title, as is shown on inscriptions.

8. *Paul...after prayer, laid his hands upon him and healed
him*: Jesus healed by laying his hands on the sick (Luke 4: 40).
Peter prayed before the raising of Dorcas (9: 40). James in
his Letter (5: 14) told his readers that, when anyone was ill,

'he should send for the elders of the congregation to pray over him and anoint him with oil in the name of the Lord'. The Spirit of Jesus could thereby act as the Holy Spirit working through his disciples—a further instance of the parallel development recurring in the growth of the early church.

10. When they left, the islanders made them many gifts and *put on board provisions for our needs*.

marks of respect: Greek, 'honours' or 'presents'. ✳

The journey from Malta to Rome

STAGE V. TO ROME

11 Three months had passed when we set sail in a ship which had wintered in the island; she was the *Castor and Pollux*
12 of Alexandria. We put in at Syracuse and spent three days
13 there; then we sailed round and arrived at Rhegium. After one day a south wind sprang up and we reached
14 Puteoli in two days. There we found fellow-Christians and were invited to stay a week with them. And so to
15 Rome. The Christians there had had news of us and came out to meet us as far as Appii Forum and Tres Tabernae, and when Paul saw them, he gave thanks to God and took courage.

✲ They left Malta some three months after the wreck. This would be about the end of February. *The 'Castor and Pollux' of Alexandria had wintered in the island*. This was probably another corn-ship on the last lap of the Egyptian run.

11. '*Castor and Pollux*': Greek, *Dioscuri*, the twin sons of Jupiter, the patron gods of sailors. The literal translation of the phrase is 'with the sign the Dioscuri'. The R.S.V. interprets this to mean 'with the Twin Brothers as figurehead'. It was probably a symbol of the gods at the mast-head. This ship, the final one that brought Paul to his destination, is the only one whose name is recorded.

12-13. The final voyage included a call at *Syracuse* in Sicily for *three days*, *one day* at *Rhegium* on the 'toe' of Italy and the trip to *Puteoli*, near Naples, *in two days* more with a favourable *south wind*.

13. *we sailed round*: or 'made a circuit' (R.V. and R.S.V.). Some manuscripts read 'cast loose'.

14. There was a church at Puteoli so Paul and his companions *were invited to stay a week* with their *fellow-Christians* (literally, 'brothers').

15. When the Roman Christians (literally, 'brothers') heard of their approach, they came out along the Appian Way 40 miles to *Appii Forum* (the Market of Appius) and 30 to *Tres Tabernae* (the Three Taverns). It must have been a great joy to Paul to see them. Rome had been reached at last. It is a very curious fact, however, that this is all we hear from Acts, of Christians in Rome. In spite of the evidence of the Letter to the Romans, when Paul actually gets to Rome itself in the story in Acts, all we hear about are Jews. ✻

IN ROME

When we entered Rome Paul was allowed to lodge by 16 himself with a soldier in charge of him. Three days later 17 he called together the local Jewish leaders; and when they were assembled, he said to them: 'My brothers, I, who never did anything against our people or the customs of our forefathers, am here as a prisoner; I was handed over to the Romans at Jerusalem. They examined me and 18 would have liked to release me because there was no capital charge against me; but the Jews objected, and I 19 had no option but to appeal to the Emperor; not that I had any accusation to bring against my own people. That is why I have asked to see you and talk to you, 20 because it is for the sake of the hope of Israel that I am in chains, as you see.' They replied, 'We have had no com- 21 munication from Judaea, nor has any countryman of ours arrived with any report or gossip to your discredit. We 22 should like to hear from you what your views are; all we know about this sect is that no one has a good word to say for it.'

So they fixed a day, and came in large numbers as his 23 guests. He dealt at length with the whole matter; he

spoke urgently of the kingdom of God and sought to
convince them about Jesus by appealing to the Law of
Moses and the prophets. This went on from dawn to dusk.
24 Some were won over by his arguments; others remained
25 sceptical. Without reaching any agreement among themselves they began to disperse, but not before Paul had said
one thing more: 'How well the Holy Spirit spoke to your
26 fathers through the prophet Isaiah when he said, "Go to
this people and say: You will hear and hear, but never
27 understand; you will look and look, but never see. For
this people has grown gross at heart; their ears are dull,
and their eyes are closed. Otherwise, their eyes might
see, their ears hear, and their heart understand, and then
28 they might turn again, and I would heal them." Therefore take notice that this salvation of God has been sent
to the Gentiles: the Gentiles will listen.'

30   He stayed there two full years at his own expense, with
31 a welcome for all who came to him, proclaiming the
kingdom of God and teaching the facts about the Lord
Jesus Christ quite openly and without hindrance.

✻ Verse 16 is the last occasion when a verb in the first person
plural is used in the narrative but this particular source may
well run through to the end with Luke as well as Paul in
Rome. Some manuscripts add that 'the centurion delivered
the prisoners to the *stratopedarch*', the officer in charge of the
camp or the commander of the praetorian guard. It is possible
that this officer was the *princeps peregrinorum*, the commander
of the officer-couriers from abroad (*peregrinus*), of whom
Julius may have been one (27: 1), rather than the Praetorian
Prefect himself. Paul was left in charge of a soldier but
allowed to lodge by himself.

17–19. Following in Rome his usual pattern elsewhere,

Paul addressed himself as soon as possible to the *Jewish leaders.* He asserted emphatically his loyalty to Judaism at all times, and yet the Jews in Jerusalem had *handed* him *over to the Romans.* They could find *no capital charge* (literally, 'no cause of death') against him, but the Jews were so insistent that he *had no option but to appeal to the Emperor,* even though he had no *accusation to bring against* his *own people.*

20. Paul claims that he is *in chains* for *the sake of the hope of Israel,* i.e. the messianic hope, of which the hope of the resurrection was naturally a part (see his defence before the Sanhedrin in 23: 6).

21–2. It seems strange that the Jews in Rome had so little knowledge of events in Judaea. Was it simply that they did not wish to know, and so kept themselves well away from any reports that might lead to trouble and inconvenience for them? Already in the reign of Claudius, an edict had been issued 'that all Jews should leave Rome' (18: 2), which may well have been owing to trouble with the Christians (see note on 18: 2). The Letter to the Romans is sufficient evidence for the existence of a considerable Christian community in the city (but see note on 28: 15 above). In view of likely complications it was better for orthodox Jews to remain in ignorance. Thus no *report or gossip* to Paul's *discredit* had reached them. Nonetheless, Paul was a Pharisee of education and standing and it would be worth their while to hear his *views* on *this sect* for which *no one* had *a good word.*

21. no *report or gossip*: literally, no one 'reported or spoke any evil about you'.

22. *this sect*: Greek, *haeresis,* from which 'heresy' comes (see note on 24: 14).

no one has a good word to say for it: literally, 'everywhere it is spoken against'.

23. At Paul's invitation the Jews came to his house *in large numbers.* He spoke at length and with emphasis *of the kingdom of God,* i.e. the reign of God as foretold in the Law and the prophets and as revealed in the life and work of Jesus as the

Messiah. With a Jewish audience Paul invariably referred to the Law and the prophets for evidence.

as his guests: the Greek permits of this translation and equally the R.V. and R.S.V. 'into' or 'at his lodging'.

24–5*a*. Despite a day's discussion (verse 23) no agreement was reached. *Some were won over by his arguments; others remained sceptical.*

25*b*–7. Paul's final comment is from Isa. 6: 9–10, which Matthew quoted when Jesus was speaking to his disciples on the use of parables (Matt. 13: 14–15). Thus the Holy Spirit, in the words of Isaiah, summed up Israel's repeated refusal to see and understand God's will for them. Here in Rome it was the same. The quotation would therefore seem to be an explanatory comment in the early church designed to deal with the problem of the lack of response of Israel.

28. Since the Jews refused to listen, *this salvation of God has been sent to the Gentiles*, who will. This is the whole burden of Luke's great work. The mission to the Gentiles had been foretold by Simeon (Luke 2: 32). The gospel narrative led up to Israel's rejection of the Messiah, as Stephen reminded his hearers (7: 52). Therefore, it is now the Gentiles' turn and they will accept the message (cf. 13: 46, at Pisidian Antioch; 18: 6, at Corinth; 22: 21, in Jerusalem; 26: 20, in Caesarea and now 28: 28, in Rome).

(29) Some manuscripts add, 'After he had spoken, the Jews went away, arguing vigorously among themselves'.

30–1. For two years Paul lived in Rome *at his own expense* or 'in his own hired dwelling' (R.V. and R. S.V. footnote), welcoming *all who came to him*. He taught *the facts about the Lord Jesus Christ* and so proclaimed the reign of God through his Messiah (see note on 28: 23).

There is a thrill of joy for Luke in these last two verses, that, not only had the gospel of *the Lord Jesus Christ* (the only time in Acts that the full title is used) reached Rome, but also Paul was able to preach it there *quite openly and without hindrance*. ✡

✡ ✡ ✡ ✡ ✡ ✡ ✡ ✡ ✡ ✡ ✡ ✡ ✡

'I AM A FOLLOWER OF THE NEW WAY' (24: 14)

Whenever a reader has finished Acts and thought about it carefully, and then says with Paul, 'I am a follower of the new way', Luke has achieved his purpose. In Acts 1: 1 he addressed this part of his work to Theophilus as he had done at the beginning of his gospel. His purpose was the same—'to give you authentic knowledge about the matters of which you have been informed' (Luke 1: 4). He was determined to convince Theophilus that 'the new way' was the 'way of salvation' (16: 17). The slave-girl at Philippi knew it when Paul and his friends proclaimed it. The same challenge is presented to the reader of Acts. To make his own decision he must approach the challenge as Theophilus did. He must be an informed person, with a critical mind, yet ready to be convinced if the evidence is sound.

The Old Testament proclaimed the way of God through Israel's experience in history. Those who followed this way were revived and restored. 'An high way shall be there, and a way, and it shall be called The way of holiness' (Isa. 35: 8). For Luke, the new Israel would follow the new 'way' that John prepared (Luke 1: 76–7) and along which Jesus was the guide. 'Can one blind man be guide to another?' Jesus said, 'Will they not both fall into the ditch? A pupil is not superior to his teacher; but everyone, when his training is complete, will reach his teacher's level' (Luke 6: 39–40). Isaiah's prophecy had been fulfilled. 'Yet shall not thy teachers be hidden any more, but thine eyes shall see thy teachers: and thine ears shall hear a word behind thee, saying, This is the way, walk ye in it' (Isa. 30: 20–1). Luke, in his gospel, described this way with Jesus as the guide and teacher. In Acts the Christian follows the same way with the Holy Spirit as his constant companion and friend. 'You will receive the gift of the Holy Spirit', said Peter to the crowds at Pentecost. 'For the promise is to you, and to your children, and to all who are far away, everyone whom the Lord our God may call' (2: 38–9).

In his commentary on Luke's Gospel in this series E. J. Tinsley refers to the picture of Jesus in this gospel as 'essentially a journeying figure' (p. 209). In Acts the comparable picture is of essentially a journeying church. The pattern of the gospel story is repeated again and again in Acts. The way of the church is the way of the Spirit of Christ. When Jesus was wedged in the crowds on his way to Jairus' house 'a woman who had suffered from haemorrhages for twelve years...came up from behind and touched the edge of his cloak, and at once her haemorrhage stopped' (Luke 8: 43–4). When the apostles passed through the streets of Jerusalem 'the sick were actually carried out...and laid there on beds and stretchers, so that even the shadow of Peter might fall on one or another as he passed by;...and all of them were cured' (5: 15–16). The same pattern of healing was experienced by Paul in Ephesus, for 'when handkerchiefs and scarves which had been in contact with his skin were carried to the sick, they were rid of their diseases and the evil spirits came out of them' (19: 12). The Spirit of Christ was abroad amongst his followers, approving their work by the same signs that Jesus himself had given.

The work of the apostles is similarly ratified by the power to restore life. Luke alone selected the raising of the widow's son at Nain as an illustration of Jesus' power over death (Luke 7: 11–17), and this example closely parallels Elijah's raising of the widow's son at Zarephath (1 Kings 17: 17–24). Jesus was the new Elijah, as the church was the new Israel (see Tinsley, *Luke*, p. 75). The apostles had their actions approved by the Spirit and Luke recounts the occasions. For Peter he chose the story of Dorcas at Joppa, when 'turning towards the body, he said, "Tabitha, arise"' (9: 40). Cf. Jesus' command to the widow's son at Nain, 'Young man, rise up!' (Luke 7: 14). For Paul he selected Eutychus at Troas, although the N.E.B. translation detracts somewhat from the parallelism by reading 'was picked up for dead' (20: 9) for the R.V. and R.S.V. 'was taken up dead'.

The presence of the Spirit in the journeying church showed itself along the way as first it did at Pentecost. By recording a selection of these occasions Luke verifies that what was taking place was in accordance with the will of Jesus. When the Holy Spirit came upon Cornelius and his friends, 'the believers who had come with Peter, men of Jewish birth, were astonished that the gift of the Holy Spirit should have been poured out even on Gentiles. For they could hear them speaking in tongues of ecstasy and acclaiming the greatness of God' (10: 45-6). When Paul arrived in Ephesus at the beginning of his long stay there, he found a number of converts who had been baptized with John's baptism and had not even heard of the Holy Spirit. After he had spoken to them 'they were baptized into the name of the Lord Jesus; and when Paul had laid his hands on them, the Holy Spirit came upon them and they spoke in tongues of ecstasy and prophesied' (19: 5-6). Although the comparison need not be overstressed, the fact that Luke records that 'altogether they were about a dozen men' (19: 7) may indicate an echo in his mind that the twelve tribes of the old Israel were reborn as the twelve apostles of the new, waiting for the Spirit in Jerusalem, and that this dozen represented the founding of the church in the important city of Ephesus.

The journeying of the early church in Acts was not only geographical. It also made its way among men of different races. It gave further proof that non-Jews were willing to accept Jesus, and made it clear that pagan superstitions were demolished in the path of the Way. The faith of the centurion whose servant Jesus healed (Luke 7: 1-10) is a pointer to the faith of that other centurion, Cornelius, whose admission into the church (10: 1-48) was such an important prelude to the general acceptance of Gentiles and to the persuasion of Jewish Christians of the rightness of the gentile mission. 'When the Holy Spirit came' upon Cornelius and his friends, 'the believers who had come with Peter, men of Jewish birth, were astonished' (10: 44, 45). But later when Peter laid all the facts before the Jerusalem church, 'their doubts were silenced. They gave praise to God and said, "This means that God has granted life-giving repentance to the Gentiles also"' (11: 18). Simeon's prophecy of 'a light that will be a revelation to the heathen' (Luke 2: 32) was being fulfilled by the Spirit in the church. Paul and Barnabas told the people of Pisidian Antioch that they had received instructions from the Lord. These were in the words of Isaiah (49: 6), 'I have appointed you to be a light for the Gentiles, and a means of salvation to earth's farthest bounds' (13: 47). As at Pisidian Antioch, so at Corinth, when the Jews opposed Paul and 'resorted to abuse, he shook out the skirts of his cloak and said to them, "Your blood be on your own heads! My conscience is clear; now I shall go to the Gentiles"' (18: 6). Nothing could hold back the Spirit. The Samaritans had been swept off their feet by the magic of Simon the sorcerer, saying '"This man is that power of God which is called 'The Great Power'"'...But when they came to believe Philip with his good news about the kingdom of God and the name of Jesus Christ, they were baptized, men and women alike' (8: 10, 12). Following the same pattern, it was because Paul was 'filled with the Holy Spirit' (13: 9) that he was able so effectually to demolish the pretensions of Elymas at Paphos. Similarly, when the seven sons of Sceva were overpowered by the man with the evil spirit shouting, 'Jesus I acknowledge, and I know about Paul, but who are you?', the Ephesians, both Jews and pagans, 'were all awe-struck, and the name of the Lord Jesus gained in honour' (19: 15, 17). Unlike Paul the sons of Sceva acted without the Holy Spirit.

The life-blood of the church, like that of Jesus himself, was prayer. Before taking the vital step of selecting his twelve apostles, Jesus 'went out one day into the hills to pray, and spent the night in prayer to God' (Luke 6: 12). When the Seven were presented to the Twelve, the apostles 'prayed and laid their hands on them' (6: 6). Before the transfiguration Jesus was at prayer (Luke 9: 28–9); before Pentecost the apostles and their friends 'were constantly at prayer together' (1: 14). When Jesus reached the Mount of Olives, he withdrew from his disciples 'knelt down, and began to pray: "Father, if it be thy will, take this cup away from me. Yet not my will but thine be done"' (Luke 22: 41–2). When Paul and Silas were arrested in Philippi and thrown into prison 'about midnight' they were 'at their prayers...singing praises to God' (16: 25). Jesus' prayer-life as recounted by Luke was a model for the church. Through the channel of prayer Jesus was in continuous touch with the Father; and through the same channel the followers of Jesus retained their contact with the Master.

So Luke, in part two of his work, saw the church reliving the life of Jesus. As he prayed, the church prayed; as he healed, so did the church; as the good news was portrayed in the life of Jesus, so it was proclaimed through the church's words and deeds. By the end of Acts the good news had reached Rome; the Spirit of Jesus was in action there. The capital of the Empire had been stormed, thus typifying the total conquest of the world which is to come. No longer was the church a hole-and-corner affair; it had reached and was now challenging the very centre of the world's life and power. The overall picture left in the mind from the reading of Acts is of a journeying church, empowered by the Holy Spirit and geared to capture the world.

A NOTE ON FURTHER READING

For further study of the text, the reader will be able to find many useful commentaries on the Acts of the Apostles in the various series that have appeared in recent years. The purpose of this Note is to help the student to fill in the background. Floyd V. Filson, *A New Testament History* (1965) provides a good general history and may profitably be read with the assistance of documents from C. K. Barrett, *The New Testa-*

ment Background: Selected Documents (1961); J. Stevenson, *A New Eusebius: Documents illustrative of the history of the Church to A.D. 337* (1965) and G. A. Williamson, *Josephus, The Jewish War* (Peguin Classics, 1960). W. M. Ramsay, *St Paul the Traveller and the Roman Citizen* (1903) still remains a delightfully refreshing book. H. J. Cadbury, *The Making of Luke-Acts* (1958) provides a valuable discussion of the relation between Luke's Gospel and Acts, and A. N. Sherwin-White, *Roman Society and Roman Law in the New Testament* (1965) a most helpful examination of the Roman and Hellenistic background. Finally, for those who read Greek, it should be remembered that the text translated in the New English Bible was edited by R. V. G. Tasker, *The Greek New Testament* (1964).

INDEX